FRAGMENTS IN PERCEPTION

poetry *pt* today

FRAGMENTS IN PERCEPTION

Edited by Natalie Nightingale

First published in Great Britain in 2002 by Poetry
Today, an imprint of
Penhaligon Page Ltd, Remus House,Coltsfoot Drive,
Woodston, Peterborough. PE2 9JX

A Catalogue record for this book is available from the
British Library

ISBN 1 86226 699 9

Typesetting and layout, Penhaligon Page Ltd, England.
Printed and bound by Forward Press Ltd, England

Foreword

Fragments In Perception is a compilation of poetry, featuring some of our finest poets. This book gives an insight into the essence of modern living and deals with the reality of life today. We think we have created an anthology with a universal appeal.

There are many technical aspects to the writing of poetry and *Fragments In Perception* contains free verse and examples of more structured work from a wealth of talented poets.

Poetry is a coat of many colours. Today's poets write in a limitless array of styles: traditional rhyming poetry is as alive and kicking today as modern free verse. Language ranges from easily accessible to intricate and elusive.

Poems have a lot to offer in our fast-paced 'instant' world. Reading poems gives us an opportunity to sit back and explore ourselves and the world around us.

Contents

David's Psalm 24

All the earth is the Lord's and everything in it,
He, the founder, had reinforced it upon the waters,
Who can go to the hills of our God
Or stand in this Holy place?
Only the pure and upright in heart,
But he will gain much blessing
And forgiveness from his Saviour,
Such inhabitants who served Him were followers like Jacob.
Oh be strong, serve Him and be lifted up,
Be as the Ancient doors, so that the king of glory may enter in,
Remember the king, the Lord of glory, the mighty one of Jacob,
Lift your heads high and call upon Him, Our Great Deliverer.
He is the King of Glory.

M Joseph

The Way Of The Cross

Christ took that awesome, cruel path,
The victim of unreasoned wrath,
He went that way for you and me,
So all the world could plainly see
His sacrifice and love defined,
A precious gift for all mankind.

   ECJ

Summertime

Trees gently swaying in a soft summer breeze
Covered in blossom and green shiny leaves
Underneath a carpet of bright coloured flowers.
A delight to behold after months of heavy showers.

Birds sweetly singing their songs all day
Winter has gone they are now back to stay.
They brighten the days and dispel the gloom
Life is much better now it's nice and warm.

Rosanna Davis

Christmas Gift
(This is a true story)

That Christmas Eve she'd tramped by Arkle Beck,
On rocky tracks and mucky swampy lanes,
Climbed slippery stiles, crossed meadows soaked by rains
Of weeping weeks; a happy family trek.
But safely back in Reeth, to her dismay
She found that on those muddy miles she'd lost
Her horseshoe brooch, a golden thing embossed
With diamond and amethyst. Next day
Her sturdy daughter and her spouse declare:
'We'll take that walk again and try to find
Your jewel.' What a hope! 'I am resigned,'
She says, yet sharp eyes spot it. There it is!
Half hidden in a pool of marshy mire.
On Christmas morn, what more could she desire?

Frank G Littlewood

The Quarrel

A spoken strife is scathing, sere,
venom voiced for all to hear,
a sharpened auger boring deep,
and hours may pass before there's sleep.

But strife's unspoken, deadly smile
breeds brooding, bitterness and bile.
The ramrod bodies know no sleep,
lie side by side, in silence weep.

Harold Wonham

The Marriage Quilt

I sit and sew here in my room
Until the day's sun turns to gloom.
No longer can I see the thread
That hems the quilt to grace our bed
With love in every stitch.

You sailed a half a world away
I promised I would not delay
A patchwork quilt I would begin
To sew with thread - I'd tuck and pin
With love in every stitch.

The pattern formed from many squares
Is fashioned from life's joys and cares.
With ruffled lace on all the seams
As delicate as lovers' dreams
With love in every stitch.

A scarlet voile is from the dress
I wore - when full of tenderness
You vowed your love, I'll not forget
And so I sew our coverlet
With love in every stitch.

I ply my needle round the grey
Remembering that sodden day
Your pa's coffin we laid in silt
His mem'ry's now stored in our quilt
With love in every stitch.

My apron was a gingham red
You laughed when I did burn the bread.
And sunshine yellow from my skirt
These scraps our mem'ries do assert
With love in every stitch.

And now you're on your way to me
Across some dark and brooding sea
Holdfast the thought throughout the storm
'Neath our quilt you'll be safe and warm
With love in every stitch.

Each scrap and rag of colour bright
Throughout our lives will bring delight
With mem'ries that will never wane
All sewn fast in our counterpane
With love in every stitch.

Pamela R Dalton

Dreamer

A dreamer never really
knows
what is truth or
just suppose
he lives in hope
of joys to be
of long wished love
to set him free.

He sees true love
in one brief look
or in the pages
of a book
he yearns for one
to hold him so
as she will never
let him go.

As with all dreams
it fades and dies
until within his
dreaming eyes
a vision will come
again
to give him light
amongst the grey
to dream away
another day.

Edward B Evans

A Doggy's Tale

I'm a Labrador, my name is Sue,
I would just like to say, 'How do you do?'
Mum says you have to excuse my muddy paws
And the way I rush through all the doors.
The smell of food is what I like,
Except for fish, and I don't like pike.
The settee is the place to snooze,
Especially with my dad's smelly old shoes.
Over the quarry my dad takes me for a walk,
We like to run and play while my dad stands to talk.
With Sally, my sister, who is a border collie.
We run up and down and through the trees then hide
                                    behind the holly.
Dad calls us both, it is time to make tracks,
We have been in the pool, so we both have wet backs.
Mum is waiting with warm towels to make us dry,
Now we could be good for her if we really try.

Zoe French

Sweep

We lived in Yorkshire in earlier days
In a big caravan which suited our ways.
It was pouring with rain one wintry night,
The fire wouldn't draw, nothing was right.
When my husband came home, all in a rush,
He got the stepladder and the flue brush,
Climbed the ladder and pushed down the brush,
Pulled out the brush and the soot all came out!
Where was my husband? Without a doubt
This soot-covered object was sneezing and choking,
It wasn't a time for laughing and joking,
Then out of the soot-covered man who stood at the door,
'What do I do now?' he did me implore.

Stella Jackson

A Songbird Caged

His hands were chained
His spirit not engaged
He lay in his cell arraigned
He was a songbird caged.

Keep smiling, his jaded spirit said.
How triumph through it all?
Try eat your cake and have it!
That in the end would pall!

The days ran into weeks
Weeks into months severe
No laughter in his sunken cheeks
A heavy load to bear.

Barred windows do a mind stagnate
A grim physical reminder
A nightmare that will suffocate
Kill, not make you surrender!

So easy would it be
To end it all - yes, all
With authority to disagree.
From a high rope to hang then fall.

Right there in his cell
He beyond coercion's reach
No one at him to yell
His anguished hours to peach!

Angus Richmond

The Secretary Bird

'She is my secretary,' he said
Patting her bottom. She turned her head,
A glossy-haired, sweet young thing;
Had him on a piece of string.

His ego, so great in his head,
Let him forget that he was wed.
Making their way up to his room,
Gave her a red rose in full bloom.

Rushing quickly towards the bed,
Nothing more could then be said.
Suddenly, rang his mobile phone;
Urgent call from the wife at home.

Hazel Mills

New Uniform

I am a copper on the beat
A new uniform I've just got
Designed to make me look quite smart
But I think they've lost the plot

My jacket is a brilliant yellow
I stand out like a traffic light
No longer do I sneak up on crooks
For my outfit is too bright

Huge pockets adorn my trousers
But the bottoms look like flares
They really do need taking in
Surely there's somebody who cares

My bell bottoms flap in the breeze
But the hips and thighs are tight
I cannot even stand and breathe
Let alone arrest or fight

I look like a Keystone Cop
In the uniform I am wearing
I pray that I can change my clothes
Before they end up tearing!

But, until then, I'll walk about
With my trousers flapping in the breeze
The jackets are so short and snug
I dare not even sneeze

I'll stand there in the High Street
Like a huge hazard light
Please don't comment on my clothes
I know I look a sight!

Sarah Patterson

Strangers In The Spotlight

We were invited to the reception
Of the wedding of some friends, Tony and Sue,
Many, many years ago,
We can laugh now but then we were
So embarrassed at what we'd done.
We arrived in our best bibs and tuckers,
Not a hair out of place,
The best man and head bridesmaid
Met us at the hotel reception.
We shook hands, exchanged pleasantries,
They got us a drink,
Placed our wedding gift with the others.
We happily mingled with the other guests,
Jan was keen to see the bride in her dress,
I was happy to mingle, wedding dresses all seem
Similar to me, more or less.

It slowly began to dawn on me
That we didn't know a soul at this reception,
Which was strange, I was about to tell Jan this,
When the master of ceremonies called 'Ladies and gentlemen,
Please be upstanding for the bride and groom, Tony and Sue.'
In sped the happy couple under the spotlight to much cheering
                                                            and clapping,
We stood rooted to the spot, bright red with embarrassment,
For we'd never seen them before,
I dug our invitations from my pocket to see
We were due at the Durley Dene Hotel,
But we were at the Durley Hall Hotel.
Whoops, big, big, whoops.
We quickly edged our way out smiling,
Grabbed our wedding gift as out we tore,
Hailed a taxi to the Durley Dene Hotel, telling everyone what
                                                            had happened.
They just laughed at our state and fell about the floor.

P J Littlefield

Ode To Gorgonzola

I'm a lover of cheese, though it fills the breeze
With an unwashed sock aroma.
Especially 'Gorgy', which laid out my Corgi
In a swoon, which was close to a coma.

The timorous mouse wouldn't enter a house
With a trap Gorgonzola baited,
For the fumes would invade every mouse house he made,
Even though double glazed and gold plated.

It's teeming with life as it slides off my knife
And proceeds across the table.
Now it's off 'cross the floor, as it heads for the door,
With me following as fast as I'm able.

The parrot gives a lurch as it falls off its perch
And buries his head in the millet,
And my brave battling Tom looks as though to say, 'Mom?'
If that thing's alive, shall I kill it?'

I say, 'No, my brave moggie, for it's all wet and soggy,
Though it's not good for pussies or mices,
But I'll settle its fate, before it's too late,
It will end up between two thick slices.'

Hilda Jones

Time Takes Its Toll

When you're young and in your prime
You think you'll stand the test of time

But when you're old at fifty-two
You wonder where the years went to

But in your mind you are still young
You feel that you're still twenty-one

You wish that you were twenty-two
With all your life ahead of you

Your body says you're sixty-one
You can no longer wear a thong

Your boobs they droop down to your waist
You can no longer win a race

With skin that's wrinkled, eyes so dim
You even have a double chin

And so as all the years fly by
You often say oh why, oh why

Just can't I dance the night away
Just like I did in younger days?

My mind it wants to run and play
My body says, no not today

But if I live to ninety-two
I don't know what I'm going to do

Instead of driving in my car
I'll put my teeth into a jar

Instead of being young again
I'll settle for a Zimmer frame.

Kathleen South

Coincidence Or Telepathy?

Sitting in Dave's room one day,
The rain outside was pouring,
Killing time and boredom
I did a little drawing.
The picture was a male's face,
Someone I didn't know,
I'd only barely finished it
Before we had to go.
The face was framed with dark brown hair,
The chin it had some stubble,
I had no idea back then
I'd meet my drawing's double.
I called the person Alex,
The first name in my head,
I put him in my pocket
And then headed home to bed.
Three months later Alex arrived
And was introduced to me,
I'd forgot about my drawing
I guess quite easily,
But then one night I cleared my coat
And guess what I should find?
A picture of our new found friend
Just like I'd read his mind!

L Berry

First Tattoo

What possessed me at the age of fifty-two
To go ahead and get my first tattoo
Was it the heat of the Spanish sun
That scrambled my brain to have it done?

Excuse me! There's no need to scream or shout
I'll tell you quietly how this came about
I know you are curious and wonder why
I suffered the agony of the coloured dye.

In Torremolinos we were strolling one day
When I spied a tattoo sign down an alleyway,
Maybe it's always been a dream of mine
To be etched for life with a nice design.

We slowly browsed through the books inside
Finding it difficult at first to decide,
Until I saw an eagle full in flight
I new instantly that would bring me delight.

So an appointment was made there and then
Was my mind fuddled, perhaps lacking oxygen?
I'd committed myself, no turning back now
The macho image had to prevail somehow.

All too soon time passed, zero hour came
Then a lifetime later my leg felt aflame,
The eagle is alive, now it wings free
That's the tale of how it came to be.

George S Johnstone

Funny Things

Visual impairment can cause quite a stir,
I've fallen over many a chair,
Put on shirts back to front.
I've walked into walls and bounced off a door
And tripped over things left on the floor.
I walked into a post and that caused some mirth
And seen all the planets in the universe.
Such laughter I've caused and the things I have done,
I tripped over the cat and fell on my bum.
And complained one time that my shoes were too tight,
No wonder, the right's on the left and the left's on the right.
What laughter that caused I can say.
Some things you do whether sighted or not,
No need to be embarrassed or feel such a clot.
If it raises laughter, so what?

Tom Usher

One Woeful Wednesday

'It's knackered,' I said
Lucy nodded her head
as we gazed at the till in dismay.
The receipt roll was jammed
no mechanic to hand
Val said, 'Alec may yet save the day.'
So we gave him a call
'cause he's good after all
with machinery and all that stuff
and he didn't delay,
he came down straight away
but his expertise wasn't enough.
When Val tried the 'Z' read
well, it made the heart bleed
for I'd left off the ribbon cassette.
It was worse than we'd feared
as no printout appeared
I broke out in an icy-cold sweat.
What the hell would Steve say
when he came in next day
and discovered the state of affairs?
Would strong words make us blush?
Would we all get the push?
Would we all have to pay for repairs?
There was naught to be done
except close up and run
to some refuge away from this sorrow,
where we'd hopefully sleep
undisturbed, while we keep
praying things will turn out right tomorrow.

Ron Beaumont

Valentine's Day: Life Is A Stage

How could you
Walk on to the
Platform
And blank me
From your sight.
You passed me by
Twice,
Before seeing your
Wife on to the
Train;
And where did we
Sit,
But in the same
Carriage,
And where did
We end,
But in the
Same theatre,
Where a green set
Turned a green thought
Into a green shade.

D Harmin

Maybe It's Me

I go for wanderings with my pa,
We find a rock to sit upon
And gently let the water cool our aching feet -
'Hey Dad! My shoes are floating off!'
I go to do some swimming, again with dear old pa,
And then complete with nice new Aran -
Pa is diving in to rescue me!

I turn the handle of a door -
To find it in my palm!
I pull a roller blind -
To see it tumble down!
I use a knife to cut the veg -
For the blade to snap clean off!
I turn a tap for water -
To feel the thing completely twist!
I sit upon the loo (nothing new to me) -
To end up in a heap and half a toilet either side!

Some days I do the simplest things –
Or that's how it should be,
So is it just the way that things are made?
Or maybe it's just me!

Sue Colson

Mole Mirth

A mole peeped through a little hole
And watched a gardener mow and roll.
He saw the dedicated care
And all the gardener's natural flair
With which he carried out his work -
No process did he rush or shirk.
He laboured there to dusk from dawn
To manicure his verdant lawn.
He trimmed and preened with joy and pride,
Then went to bed, well satisfied.
The mole, who felt a trifle smug,
Went down below and dug and dug.
Then, with a wicked shrug of mirth
Bedecked the lawn with heaps of earth!

Joan Tompkins

Friday Shop

It was on a Friday morning
When I set out to shop
Breezing along the main highway
I was forced to stop.

A long queue of cars
Heralded traffic lights to heed
It was the flood defences
Which put a damper on my speed.

When the green light showed
I did not complain
As I overcame the hazards
Of the single lane.

After running over sleeping policemen
Then I had to embark
On finding an easy space
For my car to park.

I saw there was one waiting
By the entrance door
Where I nipped in smartly
In case someone got there before.

Trolleying round the supermarket
Is a hazardous game
Everyone should get out of the way
It really is a shame.

Arriving at the shelf you want
They've stacked it up too high
And on your toes you cannot reach
However hard you try!

Anything that comes in rolls
Can easily tumble down
Bringing others to follow
Making you feel like a clown!

Easter eggs are tricky
Another balancing act
And if you drop them this time
They'll break and that's a fact.

Joyously I'm homeward bound
Then oh, woe is me!
What do I find at my front door
But a windswept, fallen tree!

Barbara Fosh

Mother's Parrot

Mum's parrot had to be 'Polly' but we called it horrible names,
a girl, or a boy was our question so it couldn't take part in our games;
no one found out for a long time and we checked for
an egg every day
we watched for a year and still nothing, so us kids said,
'Give it away.'

But Mother was proud of her parrot, it lived in a cage in the hall
and Father had fixed up a bracket so it hung from a hook on the wall,
she would polish the cage almost daily and put in
fresh water and seed,
then stretch paper across at the bottom and finish
the rest of her deed.

She'd slide out the base from its groovings, then the Brasso
she'd put to the test,
but the Vicar came calling one morning, before she could
finish the rest.
Now this parrot was into aerobics, from perch down to base
she would vault -
then land with her feet on the bottom and slide to a
nerve-racking halt.

The rest I try not to remember, the paper seemed suddenly thin -
and Polly dived through all the 'Methodist Times'
and fell down five feet - *on her chin.*
The language was not very pleasant with words taught by
brothers and me,
it was through this 'Divine Intervention'
that proved that the '*she*' was a '*he*'.

Jim Pritchard

A Funny Thing Happened

A funny thing happened to me today
And I feel I should tell you without delay!
I leapt out of bed to answer the phone,
And then I discovered I wasn't alone!

A very strange noise from the wardrobe I heard,
So I stood quite still - not uttering a word!
And if I am honest, I was really quite scared,
And to move an inch - I never dared!

Two beautiful eyes from a round face appeared,
Leaving me feeling, I must add, most weird!
I really can't say who was the most surprised,
And the ring of the phone? Yes - had suddenly died!

For in my haste to investigate the strange sound,
And wondering of course what I might have found,
I had clearly ignored the ring of the phone,
So when I re-dialled, I just heard a groan!

'Why didn't you answer?' an abrupt voice said,
'Because an enormous tiger's leapt onto my bed!'
Such exaggeration, I hastily thought,
This is a story not easily bought!

And the voice exclaimed, 'Are you sure you're alright,
Such a scary experience, must have given you a fright!'
Now I had to admit, before I elaborated even more,
Well alright, it was only the tabby cat from next door!

Carol Edney

Child

A human gesture that will never age or be conceived
As a young child holds aloft a cup, that is now clean.
An empty shell, a rotted core black and burned
For the fire engulfed the once proud home.
Cracked windows no longer clean,
No longer sparkling, no more gleams.
Yet in amongst this dismal scene
A tiny child, a parent's dream
Within her hand, a cup now cleaned.
Her face as dirty as the chair on which she stands,
'It's clean now Mum. This can be saved.'
The message clear as thoughts of despair unwind.
A human gesture that will never age or be conceived
As a young child holds aloft a cup, that is now clean.
New hope born from the ashes and remains
As the child reminds us that we still have our lives.
A tear is born instead of a joyous smile
But there is still a reason to see her side.
What she did was not to make us laugh
But instead to prove what life is worth.
To see beyond the surface, look deeper inside
To see the beauty that everything holds within.
Or look at it again. What did she want to say?
Those material possessions can be left behind.
That a fire cannot destroy the soul within
Or the bond that makes us a family.
A human gesture that will never be explained
As a young child holds aloft a cup, that is now clean.

A M Williamson

Feathers
(Dedicated to my dear friend Bryan H Leyland)

The house was so quiet, the night oh so still,
no one around, no one to see.
He pushed hard with his beak, the door opened wide,
Bobby the cockatiel flew out with glee.
Soon he was bored, flying around,
up to the ceiling and down to the ground,
so he pecked and pecked at cushions and pillows,
one by one.
Prince the dog decided to join in,
pulling and tugging, they both had such fun.
Now Bryan came home from the theatre that night,
oh dear! What a surprise!
The small living room, left so smart and clean,
resembled a white winter snow scene!
Feathers by the thousands had floated around,
then softly like snowflakes, had covered the ground.
Bryan stood there shocked, could hardly believe his eyes,
Bobby and Prince knowing that they had done wrong
went quickly away to hide.
Bryan was hopping mad now,
in a really frightful rage,
but it really was his fault because
he had not secured the door to Bobby's cage.

Dorothy Chadwick

The Missing Girdle

My mum had lost a girdle
She'd searched for it high and low
When did she last have it?
Where would a girdle go?

She checked the laundry basket
The washing machine as well
She searched bedroom drawers and wardrobe
And finally said farewell

But all became apparent on a visit to the loo
When she found instead of one girdle -
                  She was actually wearing two!

Ann Thornton

Funny-Farm Fishery

Luncheon was taken at a quarter to one
though nobody knew where it went.
The fellow behind me decked out in dun
looked exceedingly drab, like a tent.
He maundered around for most of the day,
then voted for change and got spent.

Tea was no better,
all warm, damp and brown in a cup.
The woman who served it
lost four hands of crib,
three shillings, two teeth and gave up.

It's good sitting here with little to do,
nobody dashing about.
Nine patients caught 'flu
and ten got the bends
diving down in the bath catching trout.

I expect when it's over
they'll send us lot home
to drive all our relatives spare.
Losing luncheon is worse
than boiling the phone
and that's the reason
that mine stuck me in here.

Jim Rogerson

Slug School

Now listen well you sluglets,
Take good note of what I say:
Those two giggling at the back
Could soon come to rue the day.

Your teachers have informed you
Of the treasures to be found
When once you leave the safety
Of our ancient breeding ground.

On warm days it's important
That you curb your appetite,
Until the hour for grazing
In the middle of the night.

If those young slugs don't listen
I'm afraid there is no doubt
That we'll find their sun-dried bodies
When the rest of us go out.

When we go out to forage
There's a minefield to be crossed.
Walk behind in single file:
I want no one to be lost.

This picture shows a landmine;
It's a chemical, you see:
Touch it with your glistening skin
And you die - in agony!

And then there are the beer traps,
Tempting you young slugs to sin:
You won't get back out again
Once the drink has lured you in.

So come now to attention,
Let me see a nice straight row:
All of slugkind looks to you.
Are you ready? Off we go!

Pamela Sanders

What A Bargain

I bought some boots eleven years ago
Because they were going cheap.
Some were small, some were right,
But I still squeezed them on my feet.
However, I decided to use the small ones first,
So off I went a marching
To give them such a twirl,
To the local neighbourhood shop,
Which is not far from here.
There I stood all pretty
Awaiting to be next,
Then imagine to my amazement,
My boots turned right to left.

So there I stood all innocent
Of my real, silly plight.
Mind you, it is worth a mention
They then were not so tight.

A E Jones

The Last Laugh

As I walked I slipped on some ice
it wasn't funny, nor was it nice.
But people just stood and laughed
I looked on them as daft.
It could have been serious
I could have ended up in a heap
But they found it funny,
aren't people really cheap?
What amuses some folk
is enough to make you weep.
Anyone who laughs at others' misfortune
could be referred to as a creep.
So I hope some mishap befalls them
when they are sound asleep.
They will be on the receiving end
and that will drive them round the bend.
To have the last laugh
is what I intend.

S Glover

When Spring Sprung

Almost without warning spring had sprung
signalling the garden year had begun,
slowly awakening from a long winter's sleep
new plans and promises we'd try to keep.

For we'd planned a make-over for our back yard,
the old garden being shown that famous red card,
but the problem was we just didn't have a clue
could gravel and decking really make it brand new?

Then an idea came from something we'd seen
one cold winter's night on our telly screen,
and for the next two months from that small bud
a spectacular plan grew, for our bit of mud.

The day work started and in true Ground Force style
dark clouds appeared and it rained for a while,
but that in itself was a help you see
for it ended the dilemma of where the pond would be.

So as I raise a glass to that well-known team
with the inspiration to create reality from dream,
and as I wipe yet another tear from my eye
I ask brass band music . . . why Alan . . . *why?*

J R Hirst

Ouch!

This morning started really well
As you can plainly see.
Stood on the dog and down I fell
And spilt my cup of tea.

The boiling liquid soaked the cat
Who screeched and ran away,
But that was not the end of that,
It was an awful day.

I left the house and shut the door
Then saw I had no key.
Slipped on the path, fell to the floor,
Torn tights and bleeding knee.

I struggled to my feet again,
Then slowly crossed the street.
The bus went past, down came the rain,
I've odd shoes on my feet.

Decided I would go back home,
Today is not for me.
Fell over next door's garden gnome
And scraped the other knee.

I'm tucked up safely in my bed
And this is where I'll stay.
I've just leaned back and banged my head,
I'm fed up with today!

Kaz

So Hip, Happy
(For Costas and his so hip, happy staff of the Goldstar, Tarbock Road Huyton)

She worked in a chippy once so hip, happy,
But she wasn't a cook
Nor did she look like her father's son.

I met her serving counter
Down at the Gold Star,
Her face covered in grease
From the fish and chips
And I blurry-eyed,
Fresh from the local jar-a-jar, jar.

You'd have had to have been there
To catch the moment
For despite her surround
She looked as beautiful
As any model or movie star
Could astound.

The food . . .
Was something else too.
Prepared and served
By Costas and his . . . so hip, happy . . . crew.
Be it:
> Fish and chips,
> Made to order pizza,
> Pie and mushy peas,
> Kebab,
> Take-away, curry meal.

The quality of, would more than match
The service of the staff
With their so hip, happy . . . zeal.

Malcolm Peter Mansfield

Catnaps

I love my little catnaps in the comfort of my chair
Stretching out my tiny paws with that sleepy air
Lapping up those many luxuries without a worldly care
With room service of the very best and of course beyond compare

When each dish of dainty morsels is placed upon the floor
I'm always able to scramble down to eat a little more
And if a chunk is a little large and find it hard to ignore
I push it gently to one side as if it is a chore

And of course I love my cuddles when my paws curl round her neck
Licking her face constantly interspersed with just a peck
Sometimes she gently chides me before lowering me to the deck
And so once again the good things end - so what the heck

But I hate my constitutionals when she puts me out to walk
Especially after I've eaten well and look like fatted pork
The birds gather round to gawp at me and enjoy their bragging talk
Chirruping with expectancy and expressing their mocking thought

And when I walk away they creep up from behind
Laughing at my funny shape and being so unkind
They drive me up the garden path where peace I can never find
Knowing I can't catch them having always so well dined

And before I fall asleep while basking in the sun
And my feathered friends have found the time to further their fill
of fun
I struggle back to my favourite chair where noise I can
guarantee none
To dream about those catty things I know I should have done.

Keith B Osborne

The Kiss

The delicate emotions we feel within us
When first we experience the desires of love,
As with trembling timidity we gently and shyly,
Slowly manoeuvre our bodies into close proximity,
Eyes searching each other for approval,
Unspoken though it be, yet indicating to us
That we are both desirous
Of the physical contacts we wish to feel,
And as with gentle caution, we allow
Our fingers to caress, and lovingly explore
Each other's face,
We touch, and arms embrace,
Our lips will meet in responsive passion,
Gentle though it be, this first kiss,
Can be the one that really sets the fashion.

Bah Kaffir

A Little . . . Er . . . I've Forgotten!

When you get old like me
and take to drinking toffee,
not the stuff you buy in slabs,
but a mix of tea and coffee.
Or when you sup a Colamilk,
not one that comes in cans,
but cola with a hint of cream
poured by unthinking hands.
Or when your shoes are black and tan,
the laced one on the right
and both the shoes are different,
the left one very tight.
Or when you lose your glasses
then find them on your head.
Or try to think what day it is,
or have you been to bed.
Or put your dentures in the bin,
or 'birds the feed with bread'
it's time to stop and slowly think,
'Am I alive or dead?'

Peter Clough

On Track, Circa 2002-05-26

The train pulls out
to the cheers of the people
who wave us out.
The sunshine and light, the sparkle
and glint, the hoots
and the whistles into the wind.
The drinks and the spills,
the swoosh and the lurch.

The spin of clattering wheels,
non-stop stations lean back for
breath, sucked and inhaled.
Tunnels struck, an intake of shock,
a suspension in time, in a flash forgotten.
Bursting in colour, sound and light,
the journey draws to its conclusion.

The tannoy announces:
the train has been cancelled.
I wake from my dream
to follow the very same people
who had followed me in,
to the cheers of the people
who had waved us out.

Michael Fenton

Five Minutes Yet

Upon a cold December 28th,
I drove for sixty icy miles to church.
In this fine building was my friend to wed,
But first I needed nature's call to heed.
Alas, no haven was there anywhere,
But soon appeared a man with aged stride.
'Oh sir,' I called with firm but plaintive voice,
'Where is the nearest public toilet place?'
'About a mile,' he said in bleak reply.
My look of total resignation must
Have stirred his heart to action very well,
So prompt was invitation to his home.
A fifteen-minute walk was all it took
To make me calm and wedding-fit again.
By now the call of nature pressed my wife,
Who waited car-borne - patient, growing tense.
'Fear not,' I soothed, 'we've still five minutes yet.'

Allan Bula

Ageing Seduction

It is a sad admission
Perhaps I'm growing old,
Glancing at the short skirts
Instead of going for gold.

This state will come to all men
Only luck makes it later for some,
But there are compensations
Many problems are overcome

So ~

Admire them at all times
Doff the hat and smile,
Absence of heat under collar,
'Tis really, really worthwhile

But ~

Perhaps I'm only joking,
The world can only guess,
Of course it's a serious subject,
Have fun, goodnight, God bless!

Stan Dwight

Down The Pan!

A funny thing happed when my youngest was small,
she had a step for the toilet as she was not very tall,
and a smaller seat to fit over the seat already there -
we gave her every help possible to show our care.
Then one morning at the age of three she made a big decision
and without a word to anyone, scorned *both* seats with derision;
she used the step to mount the loo then pushed it to one side
forgetting (or not realising) the space was really wide.
Too late she found she'd fallen in, arms and legs in air,
Mum and Dad both still asleep, she thought we didn't care -
so sotto voce to start with, she increased with louder cry:
''elp . . . 'elp . . . 'elp . . .'
then,
'H e l p!' awoke us loud and high!
We ran then to her rescue, and trying not to grin
saw our youngest daughter with her legs up near her chin!
We pulled her out and hugged her, for by then she was distraught
and praised her for her bravery – tho' her efforts seemed to *her*
as nought.

I'll never forget those cries of ''*elp!*' with her aitches all but dropped,
she never forgot her aitches again, but her efforts never stopped
to master how to use the loo without falling in the gap -
she used the step *and* seats 'til she'd grown, without mishap.

Now she blushes when reminded with a gentle, kindly tease
and then at once it's put behind, her feelings to appease.
So parents, when your toddlers small learn to use the loo,
Instruct them how to shout for *help* - as this could happen to you!

Ann Voaden

A Quiet Evening

There's a niece on the phone we don't see very often
Who's been invited to go out for a meal.
At the thought of her daughters our hearts start to soften,
Baby-sitting has tremendous appeal.
On arrival they look sweet, we sort out their ages.
They're dressed in their satin 'jim-jams.'
'Please read us a story - it's only ten pages.'
Seems not long since they were in prams.

Proudly they show us their tank full of fish,
One missing since we were last here.
'It's in heaven with Granny, 'cos that's what she'd wish.'
The little one's voice is sincere.
Remembering their gran had a great sense of fun,
Can imagine her looking quite merry,
Saying, 'A fish is the last thing I want under the sun,
I'd sooner have a schooner of sherry.'

Bedtime's arrived, they're safely tucked down,
We relax thinking games did the trick.
When the door opens wide, a face as white as a clown
Announces it's feeling quite sick.
We leap to our feet but find it's too late,
There's a nasty splodge on the floor.
Child needs a cuddle, cleaning can wait -
Then the dog comes in through the door.

Chaos ensues - keep the dog from the mat!
With what do we start to mop up?
The next to come in is their curious cat,
And the patient wants water in cup.
When their mummy returns we start to explain
And can all see the funny side.
'I know what will happen if I ring again,
You'll have something on!' she cried.

Mary Jelbart

46

Fleas (Bleeding Biters)

I've been invaded by fleas
Who have no sense of boundaries.
They do anything they please,
Know no social niceties,
Jumping and jiving everywhere,
Skipping and hopping in the air,
Showing devastating flair
As they ascend each well-trodden stair.
I've bathed the cat until she almost drowned,
Whilst flea powder I've scattered all around,
But do their dead bodies lie piled up in mounds?
No! For they've found a happy hunting ground.
I vacuum night and day, 'til my carpet's worn away,
That even the dust mites have no place to stay,
But the fleas think it's a new game to play.
One jump ahead of me you might say.
Even the cat stays out of doors,
Knowing the havoc that she's caused.
From the beginning her flea collar was a lost cause.
The invaders gave it no more than a second's pause.
As the cat, her coat she bites and claws,
What on earth am I to do?
Since, I've used the spray on me too,
But each day the bloody bites appear anew.
Won't someone listen to my plea?
I'm in deep trouble can't you see
They're driving me up the proverbial tree
As like the cat, into the garden I must flee,
In desperation, a total lunacy,
Driving out by the busy, biting flea.

John Pegg

Does A Sheep Say, 'Baa'?

Oh, mosquitoes whine and bees they buzz,
Does a sheep say, 'Baa'? It never does.

Poor sheep are dim, their minds run dully,
Both fleecy coats and brains are woolly,
No thought of heaven and earth or sky
Are dreamed of in their philosophy,
Mindlessly following from here to there,
The older say, 'Arrgghh'! the younger, 'Mair'!

Oh, midges drone and flies they buzz,
Does a cow say, 'Moo'? It never does.

In fields and byres all cows concur,
To communicate they all say, 'Mer'!
And licence has been made poetical,
That cattle all say, 'Moo', phonetical,
'Oo, look,' we cry, 'a field of kine,'
To 'oo' is human, to 'er', bovine.

Oh, gnats they scream and wasps they buzz,
Does a duck say, 'Quack'? It never does.

All ends of words a duck will lop,
The Anatidaen glottal stop,
But living on marsh and tributary,
Its language at best is estuary,
So we may feed them crumbs from a paper sack,
But the only reply from a duck will be , 'Qua'!

Oh, fireflies hum and bluebottles buzz,
Does a pig say, 'Oink'? It never does.

A pig relaxes in its sty,
Content to watch the world go by,
Unlike cows, sheep and water birds,
It does not roam in flocks or herds,
But in detached domestic bliss,
Dwells in its porcine oasis,
No wonder its only oral action,
An occasional grunt of satisfaction.

Oh, insects drone and whine and buzz,
Does a cat say, 'Miaow'? - Well, yes, it does.

Barry Jones

Toasting Bread On Toasting Forks

I don't know,
You could have waited.
I came, but it
Was too late.
Such a thing
Couldn't be fated!
It is as black and
Dark as a grating
In Hell's bosom.
You might come
Soon to see
Me again:
With your relative
And the article,
But that is a
Fashion
And soot comes
Off the safer
When you've
Finished with
Your passion.
Bread is bread,
The fork's, the
Chimney too.

Nicola Barnes

Waffle Brain

I've got a head like a sieve.
I did my English in my French book.
I left my lunch at home when I went to school.
I thought it was a Tuesday when it was a Thursday.
I thought my deadline was the 4th and not the 3rd
And I'm having a bad hair day.
My twenty-four hour clock's a muddle
So I missed the bus back home.
I forgot we have no hot water
And took a cold shower.
I've lost that important letter,
And Mum's not home to cook tea.
We now have a power cut,
So it's a pot noodle with cold water.
In the shops I buy the bag of sugar with a split.
My essay is full of errors,
Even though I had spellcheck.
I almost went to school in my PJs
And I almost forgot my name.
I forgot that school finished early today
And now I'm waiting for Dad.
At home relaxing I press the TV switch on
And the whole house is gone.

Laura Sanson

During The War

Yes, a funny thing happened to me,
It was nineteen forty-three.
I had been away from Mum and Dad,
But by then things were not too bad.
I was fourteen by then and matured,
I had learned to be brave and assured.
The war was being won, it seemed,
So I had to 'start work' she beamed!
That was my auntie! I had to live in the country.
Well, there were two industries,
Being just a village near Northampton.
One produced cocoa, the other, jam.
Now both jobs involved things sticky,
With sealed cartons of cocoa tricky.
That involved using 'glue'
To make cartons to put cocoa in.
Well I chose the cocoa factory,
Not my ideal job, but, it had to be done.
So first thing next day I clocked on,
Got on fine, until that fateful day
I was dared to look out the window.
It was just a small Italian fellow.
They had a 'camp' for just a few.
Being a daredevil, but only 5ft 2,
I had to stand on a big drum.
The lid was very thin and I fell in!
This big drum was full of glue.
My shoes all sticky *and* new,
All I could cry was, 'Don't tell Mum!'

B Clark

Dry Bread

whilst making up my sandwiches one morn
i had the radio and the kettle on
how many will make up?, i thought to myself
as i turned to get the bread from off the shelf

i will have four on cheese and two on jam
then i noticed i had a tin of ham
no, cheese will do for the rest of the week
i will have the ham on Saturday for a special treat

that's the kettle ready, time for tea,
oops i forgot the milk, silly me
as i drank my tea and looked at the time
then finished making my sandwiches and thought, that's just fine

right, time for work, i thought to myself
as i put the bread (or so i thought) back upon the shelf
so off to work i went
to earn some money that i had already spent

at teatime in the works canteen
i opened my sandwich box and only dry bread was seen
oh what a mix up! my sandwiches in the house
this dry bread is only fit for a mouse
it's said that you can't live on bread alone
you're bloody right, i will raid that fridge when i get home

John R Carrey

53

The Culprit

Shall I now write in praise of spring,
Of snowdrop, crocus, daffodil?
I try - but contrive no such thing.
Pounding near, a pneumatic drill.

Depict bluebell woods if I can.
A greening of trees on yon hill . . .
In vain, because some wretched man
Still wielding that pneumatic drill.

Cherry blossom will flutter down,
Over road edge and garden spill
Through suburbia into town -
Shaken there by pneumatic drill.

To our shores birds are returning -
To fields, to woodland deep and still.
Fly here, and they'll soon be learning
How ghastly man's pneumatic drill.

Noise to terrify any bird,
None around here to chirp or trill.
I can't, myself, hear any word -
Ears blasted by pneumatic drill.

No way I'll be the first to hear
A cuckoo, though I wait until
This din dies down, because I fear
There's no end to pneumatic drill.

Should I be driven slowly mad
And my poetic output - *nil,*
Though all may shrug and say, 'Too bad!'
The culprit is – pneumatic drill.

The monstrous noise now dies away,
But so does all I mean to say.

Chris Creedon

Untitled

When I was expecting my son James,
I have to say I take the blame,
My absent-mindedness became more pronounced,
And this is my tale I now announce.

Rushing off to work one day,
I suddenly noticed to my dismay,
Instead of shoes upon my feet,
Were fluffy slippers treading down the street.

Hurried down the road, hoped no one would notice,
Marching past the curry house, the one with the name of Lotus,
Sidled in through the back staff door,
Hoped my colleagues my feet would ignore.

Luck was on my side that day,
First one in I have to say,
Hurried off to the locker room,
A spare pair of shoes residing next to a broom.

So although I could have saved my blushes,
And denied I'd forgotten to put on my galoshes,
I did admit to my memory lapse,
And watch their faces in laughter collapse.

Nicola Varmen

Sugar

Oh *why* do they have to spill sugar
All over the kitchen worktop?
Would it be so hard
To Just laden the spoon
And tip it straight into the cup?

No - spread it around seems the motto
When sweetening their coffee or tea
Or when covering a mountain of cereal
A snow-cap of sugar runs free.

Just shed a bit here
And shed a bit there
I know that they
Just do not think.

But when *I've* cleaned up for the thousandth time
And shot it straight into the sink
I do so despair to get anywhere
By asking them *nicely* to think.

It' such a small thing to worry about
I suppose that I shouldn't get cross
But if it's so easy to clear up the mess
So why then can't *they* wield the cloth!

Fiona Franklin

Growing Old Disgracefully

Who was it said that ageing should bring us peace and calm,
And if we couldn't do good turns we shouldn't do a harm,
Why should our ageing bones be consigned to rocking chairs,
When our inner thoughts and urges belie our greying hairs?

Why can't we paint the town red and raise a little hell,
Swing a wicked hip and chase the dolly-birds as well,
Do a ton-up on the motorway on an evil-looking bike,
With a blonde dish on the pillion that we really, really like?

Why can't we go clubbing on good old Saturday night,
Knock a couple back, maybe go out like a light,
Why should it be the youngsters that always have fun,
Just because it's easier for them to dance and jump and run?

I wanna don my glad-rags and forget I'm getting old,
I wanna act I'm young again and do things really bold,
I wanna live and love and really go to town,
And forget all this ageing stuff that always gets me down.

Perhaps when I get *really* old, like a century or more,
I'll see a little sense and condescend to leave the floor,
Even then, the spirit will be willing and never, *ever* weak,
It'll only be the flesh that gets so ruddy weak!

G K (Bill) Baker

Frog Tactics

It is a proven fact
That garden ponds
Do need to be cleaned out.
Delays, excuses,
Then one day
He took the plunge.
(Not literally, of course.)
The plants were moved,
The water drained,
(A pause for coffee break)
He cleaned the sides,
Then came the job he thought
Would be so easy.
Remove old pump and fountain head,
Connecting a brand new one,
But -
The pool was occupied -
A dozen frogs and more
Had other ideas than this.
Why should things change?
They formed a working party,
Their aim to stop this interfering man.
He moved them out -
They all jumped back
And sat upon the pump
And all along the pipe.
Not once, but over and again
This struggle now ensued.
Ten cups of coffee had been drunk
Before that job was done!

Roma Davies

Private John Clarke

My father was in the last war -
In the Army was he.
Sadly he had a stutter,
So the lads would take
The mickey out of him.
He wanted to get his own back
And smiled with a cunning grin,
Making them all a cup of tea
With a secret ingredient in!

Not long after,
There were soldiers standing in line -
Waiting to use the toilet,
Not like soldiers on parade.
The queues became longer -
As far as my father's eyes could see,
For he had put in Epsom Salts
Into every cup of tea!
So every soldier
Paid dearly for the price.
'I said I would get my own back,'
As he smiled with such a glee,
'That will teach you all -
If again you take the mickey out of me!'

Rachael Clarke

The Sound

In the quiet still of night
I hear a sound
That's not quite right.
Must get up
To explore
But the sound is no more.
Children all counted for
But now I have one more,
My daughter's friend
He turns out to be,
With a few clothes missing, you see.
Door is opened,
Exit made,
His clothes whizzing past him
In the rain.
Peace returns
To bed again.

Glenda Rowbottom

Dedicated To All The Parents Who Have Lost A Baby

Every day I grieve,
I grieve for my unborn baby,
My little angel who passed away
Without saying, 'Mum.'
One day, maybe?

A dark, lonely night
Follows a numb-sensed day,
Friends tiptoe on already shattered eggshells
'Cos they don't know what to say.

Night follows day,
Day follows night,
Without my little girl,
I'll never feel right.

Day by day, week by week
Comes the returning-to-normal sensation I seek.
People stop crushing shells and they talk, walk and leave,
And do you know, something funny happened the other day,
I just simply forgot to grieve.

    L Best

Me Teaspoons

Me teaspoons are disappearing,
Wonder where they go?
I know I shouldn't use 'em,
But I love my sugar so.

They say it makes you fatter
And you don't need it about,
But who would want to eat rhubarb pie
If there's no sugar about?

There'd be no honey or marmalade,
Nor any strawberry jam.
What would I put on my new-baked bread
If they got rid of all that stuff?

Didn't like the sugarcane beatings
But they must have found a way
For me to have my sugar
In this day and age.

So come on, my little teaspoons,
Don't hide and lose your job,
I want you around a bit longer yet,
Don't want to lose *my* job.

Beth Spinks

Walking In A Shadow

As I walked with my son our shadows crossed
And I began to reminisce of the time I myself had lost
I can't remember the days when my own father held my hand
I don't remember if we talked or even played in the sand.
It seems so lonely as a child when no one's there
To let you know they even care,
So I vowed to myself that this would never be
That nothing would ever be kept a secret between
                                    my children and me
And as we walked I squeezed his little hand, oh so tight,
You just don't know the feeling a father gets when his child looks
Up at him and thinks, everything is alright.
So take that walk and watch the shadows cross and you'll get
                                    the same feeling as I,
And if you're smart you won't let that feeling be his memory
                                    and just pass you by.
For memories soon fade and most thoughts just pass,
Treasure that moment, love your children, tell them so,
For you're the only one that can make that shadow last.

Raymond Earl Buchanan

Short

My godfather died;
He died in the night.
Nobody cried:
We should have worn white.

Alastair McGuiness

The Yearning

My yearning passes me
From one day to another day,
From one week to another week,
From one month to another month,
From one year to another year,
Then I fall under gloomy time,
I go to pub to smooth my yearning,
Even there I could not relax;
There the smell of the air was unbearable,
I walk out, I meet a woman that suddenly appears,
Who could unlock any heart and feed
With angelic sculpture, her passion read,
Look at me and like a magic despair,
Path so gloomy and endless.
I sat on the grass and fell asleep,
I saw Heaven full of young people,
I asked, 'May I join?' the answer was,
'Why not, we were once old,
Here, we're not young nor old, but just merry.'
I open my eyes, I see glittering sun,
Beneath me lies green grass;
Next to me a book and a pen.
I open the book: reading is like that.
Do finish your story, if you want rewards,
Then you will stop yearning.

Milan Trubarac

Off

The surface of the sea glistens in the sun.
I feel the ray of sunshine's tender touch.
I am off everything and I need to run,
To run away from former life ant hutch.

I feel the everlasting spirit around.
My soul is floating, my fetters have burst,
I catch a glimpse of a silent, divine sound -
The sound of nature, to hear it (again) I thirst.

In the horizon golden the sun has set,
And from the nearby rush takes off a swan.
Oh, I'm longing to have wings to fly with him,
To a place where life will never be torn.

Ann Kristin Muerköster

Off

Off, a word so tiny
A tiny word with many meanings.
March off, noises off and take off,
Off road, off street and off side.
Keep off the grass,
An order,
Be off,
But hopefully be back.
Fall off the ladder,
That's not good at all.
The engagement is off,
A bad and sad happening.
Be off the map
Can be good.
Be well off,
Could not be better.
Off and on
And on and off.
To finish off –
Off, a word so tiny,
A tiny word with many meanings,
Off.

Marit Clausen

The Promise

The Promise
made in cold stone air
half a century ago
out of heather hills
Caledonian water
Celtic ancient pure.
Ties that bind
Binds that tie.

The Promise
made for life
oceans crossed
time zones, cultures,
miles travelled, distances
between home, abroad,
parents lost, grief profound.
Ties that bind
Binds that tie.

The Promise
made through strength
from generations before
carried the children
through small hours
early days, happy times.
Ties that bind
Binds that tie.

The Promise
hope in the future
constancy from the past
return again to homelands
cool Scottish air
time to reflect, share.
Ties that bind
Binds that tie.

The Promise
made in faith
tested time after time
through long, demented hours
still holds true, pure
as crystal.
Ties that bind
Binds that tie.

The Promise
testimony to love
enduring, growing deeper
holds its course
bearing witness
celebrate its truth.
Ties that bind
Binds that tie.

Jane Elizabeth Hayhurst (nee Harris)

Bittersweet Season

We were all laughing so much,
that tears streamed down our faces.
Then there was a heavy shower,

distant thunder moaned sleepily.
The rain mingled with our tears,
before falling to the ground.

Like tears falling to a pillow,
for a bittersweet reason.
But showers come to an end,

the sun is never far behind.
Lifting our dampened spirits,
while lifting water to the clouds.

We were full of the joys of spring -
happy that our tears of laughter,
would rain upon another face.

Olliver Charles

The Little Sister I Did Not Know

Dear little Bridie, the darling baby sister I did not know,
With love and pride, our parents told me of your short, precious
life long ago,
How God wanted you back, an angel for His heavenly home,
A beautiful rose from His garden, you were only here on loan.
Sad and broken-hearted, our parents had to let you go,
The love and happiness you brought them, only God will ever know.
Dad bravely carried your tiny white coffin all alone,
As Mum waited to give birth to a cherished, new baby son.
A heavenly angel, you brought them messages of comfort,
peace and joy,
You told them to give thanks for this gift of a healthy baby boy.
Our parents accepted God's will and slowly learned to cope,
Later on I, your sister, was sent to fulfil their faith and hope.

Angela Moore

The Badger And More

Oh! Here we go o'er the misty hills
The haunting pipes skirling by old meal mills
Badgers and hawfinches in forest heart
Goosander and roe deer they sweetly part

In clearings of grass at dusk and dawn
The fallow among the trees while they mow the lawn
The buzzard with its resounding calls
Peregrine on the Wye valley cliffs and falls

The raven too is often seen
Crossbills calling where wild fowl preen
Rosebay, blackthorn, bramble and butterflies
Willow herb and emperor dragonflies

Grey squirrels squirming with their bushy tails
Honeysuckle by woodland paths and rails
Woodpeckers spotted on beeches and oaks
From its sett the striped head of a badger pokes.

Gina A Miller

Beyond Imagination

Caressing the essence of the intangible
    Instinct

Lifted by forces unknown
    Transient

Pastiche of intuitive knowledge
    Healing

No hiding place
    Lavender

To pass through the haze
    Magnificent

Second movement from the seventh
    Allegretto

Silent aid
    Effortless

Where fate begins, the gods end
    Faithless friend

Out of reach of the effluvia
    Elusive

Beyond the infinite.

P Brett

Storm In A Tea Cup

It was just an ordinary teaspoon,
like any other, it stirred your tea
as easily as mine. Just the same
that is till the assassin melted
its metal down and fired the bullet
it made into a president. That teaspoon
was different, that teaspoon
stirred a nation.

I'm charting the unrest
of the world we live in and how
weapons are now everyday objects
to the terrorists, as with the
twin towers attack using planes.

Vann Scytere

My Heart, My Life, My Smile

I miss you with the sensuality of lovers,
The tenderness of a kiss in the dark
Or in twilight beneath the full moon;
To have not seen you for so long
Has left me searching.
I breathe with you in my soul,
And wish for the moment upon which
There may be us joined in an eternity
Where the chalice of life may be drunk
And our hearts may be wed
In motions of love
Soulfully within you,
There-upon your sweet loving bed.

Anthony Rosato

Sun, Moon And Stars

Will there ever be an end
It just goes on and on
I dream of the sun,
Moon and the stars
To take me places
I've never been before
To open my eyes
And experience life
For myself
Will there ever be an end
Only a dream
Of the sun, moon and stars.

E A Triggs

A Shakespeare Play That I Have Seen

Unforgiven from Blighty's bloody battlefield
And kissing on the flight of cheering angels, goodbye.
The boys hath left
And put their swords aside
To forgive divine
And go from dark to light.
'Richard, my good friend, I do not understand what's going on.'
And through a sinister forest they rode.
'A leader who can rid us of this menace,
Banquo! He is brave.'

J Baird

London's Transport

London's traffic is always vile,
It takes you all day long
Just to travel half a mile.
I would use public transport
But the Underground isn't the best.
When the trains will arrive,
That's anybody's guess.
It is completely worn out,
Because it's very old.
It needs to be rebuilt completely,
But the government says
That they can't afford.
The buses are overcrowded
Because there are so few
And they are very expensive,
Both of these are true.
There will be congestion charges,
Or is that just all talk?
Then I'll ride a bicycle,
Or better still, I'll walk.

F C Pelton

One Way To God - There Are Many

There is no downside to God.
We are all One. In the stillness,
You will find your 'true being.'
In the stillness, you will hear the
Breathing of your soul - and of God.
Begin by setting aside a tiny percentage
Of your waking hours each day -
That is all it will take -
To commune once more with *Me*.
I am calling you to commune with God.

Frank Findlay

Shaping Up?

Oh dear me, what can I do?
I'm getting old and I'm feeling blue.
I really am a pathetic soul,
For this figure of mine is out of control!
My once firm tummy now ripples and sags
And my boobs seem to droop like airless flags.
Whenever I bend, my bones creak and groan
And I seem to do nothing but constantly moan!

I really must stop and give myself a shake,
For there's only so much a body can take.
It's time that I joined a fitness club.
I might get a toy boy to give me a rub!
My muscles will ache and seize up with pain
Still, I must do something ~ that fact is plain.
No doubt eating sweets will be a deadly sin,
But I'll just have to bear it if I want to be thin!

At last I've joined up, and I must have been mad.
The past few weeks have been incredibly bad.
I bend and stretch and crouch down on one knee,
'Lord help me get through this,' is my silent plea.
The music goes on, so I twist and I turn,
My bottom is raw with a carpet burn!
They don't seem to mind that I'm puffing and blowing,
So with stiff upper lip, I resolve to keep going!

Time has now passed and at last it's quite fun –
Just knowing there are others shaped like a bun.
We laugh and we joke as we go through our paces
And don't mind the sweat that runs down our faces.
To lose weight or keep fit ~ what does it matter?
Much more important is our weekly 'natter'.
By making new friends, my depression has vanished,
Those inadequate feelings, I've permanently banished!

Mary McLeod

The Wild Boar

The moon in the east
And the howl from the beast
On the forest floor,
Rampages the wild boar.
In the overwhelming darkness
There is an eerie calmness,
The boar charges again
And the face of fear falls upon men.
Deep jet-black are the skies,
Where the wild boar lies,
His husk silhouetted by the trees.
Terror makes men freeze
Because on the forest floor,
Rampages the wild boar.

I T Hoggan

The Dentist

Please don't make me go in
my teeth are really fine
I don't want him to take them
after all, these teeth are mine.

The smell it makes me sick
and the noise, it hurts my ears.
The dentist's getting closer,
my eyes are filled with tears.

The dentist gives a great big smile
and says I'll be all right,
Mum takes me closer to the door
the room gives me a fright.

But still they take me in
I don't think they really care.
They give me an injection
next I'm floating in the air.

I hear their voices talking
but I don't know what they say.
The room is spinning slowly
that means I'm on my way.

Next thing I know is I'm awake
and my mouth is pretty sore
I look around the little room
there's Mum standing by the door.

I've just been to the dentist
and I think that I'd admit
things were not so bad
it didn't hurt a bit.

J L Preston

Ups And Downs Of A Modern World

Our ambition must be to stay the course
And not turn back the clock
The numbers may have to be altered
To ensure survival on our flying rock

The future will come in stages
Be they peace or boom or war
Something unexpected?
Of that we can be sure

Two world wars behind us
Peace struggling for success
One conflict is sorted
Another springs up in its place

Berlin, Korea, Cuba
Cold days they certainly were
Israel, Northern Ireland, South Africa
Base sectarian war

War will become exhausted
Strife will be in reverse
It is as this time approaches
We will put in our best efforts.

Tim Frogman

Night Diners (Cimex Lectularius)

They were summer guests of the wall
With penthouse suites in the ceiling,
Provoked into wake by the call
From a sleeper's nasal pealing.

Their hordes then approached a well
To sample warm soup through a pore,
Some bloated full to the shell
Would fall like drunks to the floor.

Flushed red not by shame or guilt
But blood newly-drawn at the bed,
Leaving the body under a quilt
Unaware of the meal it had bled.

A restless form would awake at light
Eye the parasite foe it had fed,
Squash them flat with an angry smite
Then gag in the smell of their dead.

A donation can have its reward,
To lose blood may not mean disaster,
But I'm damned if I'd be the board
For bed-bugs housed by the plaster.

In the corners beneath the bed frame
Gorged tenants would sometimes dwell,
With the heat of a long candle flame
I returned those neighbours to hell.

How I cursed those blood-sucking diners
From the plaster with horse-hair nerve,
Did the menu list describe us minors
As main course, pudding or hors d'oeuvre?

S R Green

Anniversary

It was a hot sunny day
Your anniversary
When we took a train
To Marne La Valee
And stayed in the Euro
Hotel Santa Fe

A mouse on the train
And one at the station
Was starting to look
Like infestation

I wanted to remember
Where I was
When anyone died
But I was nowhere when anyone died

I wanted to remember
How much there was to pay
For a flight gone astray
For life gone away

I wanted to remember you
On a hot summer's day
In the driving seat
Of a pink Chevrolet
Parked by the reception
Of the Hotel Santa Fe

Instead I remembered
This Dublin café
On a grey windswept day
A breakfast gone cold
And a newspaper
Telling unwanted
World news for the day.

G T Sumner

Love

My love, you brightened up my life
Took away all daily strife,
For so much happiness came to be
Because of love, between you and me.
But, too soon, that love was lost
And I am left to count the cost.
All that remains is the memory
Of how wonderful it used to be,
But, true love can never die
And so I sincerely say, that I
Will cherish that love so it will be
With me, right to eternity.

Joyce Metcalfe

Quality Time?
(Or a trainee counsellor's blues)

I'm learning to listen
In the way that I should
I'm understanding and tolerant
And my empathy's good.

I know how to clarify
Paraphrase and reflect,
I'm supportive and focused
And your views I respect.

I'm attentive and genuine
Responsive, sincere.
I ask the right questions
Till your fears become clear.

I'm trustworthy, flexible
Reassuring and kind
Always tactful and sensitive
Never speaking my mind.

But with so many qualities
How come *I'm* so blue?
Here - move over a minute
And *I'll* talk to *you!*

Betty Nevell

The Battery Hen

Oh I am a battery hen
And what a life I live,
I'm cooped up all day
In this barbed-wire cage
And the roof on my head is a sieve.
Wanna know what I do
As I sit here alone?
Well I'll tell you, I will,
But I don't mean to moan.
So I wait, laying eggs,
Till my bottom is sore
And I peck at my food
And I scratch, what a bore!
I've laid eggs all my life
And I know what is next,
I'll be plucked, stuffed and roasted,
Gosh that makes me feel vexed.
And I think to myself
As I gaze at the net
I won't live much longer
That you can bet!
I won't go to hell though,
'Cos I ain't been bad.
Yep, I'm a battery hen
And what a life I've had.

E Farrar

National Hero

They stride around the ring
Heads held high with pride
Muscles ripple under taut skin
Bodies honed to perfection
Minds focused on the task
Ready for the day's action
This day might be their last
While the spectators look on
Electing their own favourite
A hero to beat the rest
Victor, champion
At least for today.

Geraldine Laker

A Song

I have reached out and touched
Now I know I can tell
That only a poem can sing
I cannot see as others see
Nor feel the touch of the wind
No longer walk on soft green turf
No hear the song of the birds
All quickly vanished when the curtains fell
Then clouded my vision of life
But I can feel and touch

My chair, soft cushions to help me sleep
Then dream of those I have loved
What more can anyone wish
It all seemed bad when I'd lost it all
Continue believing, it's really all worthwhile
Don't give in to painful spells
Let them all fly away
Blow them like feathers
They will soon disappear
No matter what happens
Dreams become sweet
Then all's right with the world.

Winifred Parkinson

Lines Written On Hearing Of The Death Of Barbara Castle (1910-2002)

Don't feel embarrassed if you cried
For there were many felt bereft
On hearing the red queen had died,
Towering icon of the Left.

She led campaign for women's rights,
Crusader with a tongue of fire.
A life of arguments and fights.
And she had no plans to retire.

Her long career in politics:
It kept her in the public eye.
Could handle both bouquets and kicks.
But all heroines have to die.

Red queen has left the battleground.
She fought right to the very end
Against injustices she found.
And she died the pensioners' friend.

F G Ward

A Mother's Abused Love

Is there such a thing as an abused mother
When one's own children make her suffer?
I feel so hollow and empty inside
Many nights I sit and cry
Do I deserve all these lashing tongues
Of one's own daughter and adult sons
Accused of being an uncaring mother
Finding excuses to make you suffer
The insults go on, night after night
All they ever do is fight
They squeeze the life from your aching heart
Like poison on the end of a dart
Letting you know just what they feel
Your sanity your children steal
Saying they wish that you were dead
Laying you in your watery bed
Vile, nasty words that pierce the soul
You're a mother, after all this is your role
To your tears and unhappiness they are blind
Not knowing the meaning of the word kind
Never a kiss or a comforting arm
Destroying you with mental harm
No thanks for the years you sacrificed
Bringing them up, protecting their lives
No longer does your home belong to you
So full of bitterness, hateful gloom
I love my children with every heartbeat
Even when they make me weep
But I pray each day to be released
From the name 'Mother' and given some peace.

J M Parsons

Feathery Friend

I am a little bird
Sitting in the tree,
Hiding in the branches,
Peeping out where no one can see.

Listening with my little ear,
Watching if the coast is clear
To see what folk throw on the ground,
Sure that puss is not around.

All my friends fly down with me,
Finding tit-bits for their tea.
Bread and cake crumbs to eat,
Lovely nuts a special treat.

A little drink for us is there,
Showing that folk really do care,
Then all the little birds like me
Will sing our thanks so merrily.

Winifred Brasenell

The Timeless Dance . . .

When tired children close their eyes
All their toys come out to play,
And once again the room is filled
With laughter and gaiety.

The sleeping children do not hear
The dancing and the merriment
For no one but the toys will know
And so the children sleep content.

One by one they all awake,
Elves and fairies, queens and clowns,
Fairytale characters, storybook friends
All the toys from Toy Town.

Teddy bears and dancing dolls
Soldiers decked in uniforms red
Cowboys and Indians, horses and all
With big, proud elephant marching ahead.

The band turn out with flutes and drums
The music calling them to dance,
Great fun is had by one and all
As the figures merrily prance.

But time waits for no man, not even for toys
And soon the next morning will break
So still full of joy and still dancing in time
The toys must return to their crates.

And that is the reason that every toy
Wears a happy and secretive smile
For whenever their young friends fall into sleep
The toys will be dancing in style!

Avril Ann Weryk

94

Edgy

Taking a short cut through the park,
A little nervous, as it's getting dark,
I can hear people, which makes me bolder,
And I keep looking over my shoulder,
But there doesn't seem to be anyone about,
Yet I am sure I heard somebody shout.
Then an old lady came into view,
She said, 'Don't be scared, I will look after you.'

She walked me to the park gate,
Then she seemed to hesitate,
She touched my face and gave me a smile
And told me she would have liked to stay for a while.
When she left, I felt so sad
But I knew I had seen her before,
Arriving home I went upstairs and opened my top drawer,
I found her in my photo album,
A baby then with my Great Gran,
I touched her face, she is always there for me,
I love you always Nan.

Maureen Arnold

To Our Micky

Micky became a stray
When her people left her and moved away.
I heard her miaowing night after night,
The poor little cat was in a terrible plight.
When I bedded down our horses
And went to get their hay
I put my hand under the tarpaulin sheet
And had a fright right down to my feet,
For there lay Micky, really weak.

Micky became our stable cat
She had a warm box amongst the tack
And repaid us by clearing away every rat.
The years rolled on and then one day
We moved our horses far away,
The tackroom dismantled, the field lease expired
So we decided Micky should be retired
To a life of luxury in our house she should be
She settled in and was well fed,
At night she snuggled against her master on his bed.

She loved and adored him, this master of hers,
And would have followed him all over the Earth.
Then one day, we too moved away,
To a little cottage amongst the hills.
Micky played and explored as only a cat can
But with always one eye on her favourite man.

Their friendship was more than the eye could see
They had an inner bond,
Of which they would never be free
The cat loved her master, the master his cat

96

And up to Micky's end it stayed like that.
She is still with us, in spirit, I mean
For many a time a black shadow can be seen
To check on her master to see he is all right,
Then she quietly slips away,
Into the silent night.

Erika Rollinson

Sonnet

I wept as I held my loved one dead
Such peaceful days we once enjoyed
At my side he rests his weary head
In sickness and in health we both obeyed
Ours the love match all should know
Completely faithful to each other Lord
To each other's wishes we would bow
Never with each other were we bored

At spring and summer's glorious break of day
And birds a-singing in the sun's warm rays
Brought us a life which joined our way
As we walked through life's brightly and lovely maze
My love and I will meet on yonder shore
And I shall weep, I shall weep no more.

Janet Cavill

Suddenly It's Spring

Over woods and hills and parkland
Behold a sight so rare
When Mother Nature waves her wand,
There's magic in the air.

Old 'Barren Earth' has come to life
Survey the wondrous scene,
Snowdrops, crocus, bluebells,
Burst through their leaves of green.

The sun has warmed the earth once more
A 'New World' all around
Birds are singing songs of love
Their ever-mating sound.

And in their nests their fertile eggs
Are cracking one by one
Beginning life with squawks and squeaks
They know that spring has sprung.

Fields and hedgerow turned to green
There's newborn lambs at play.
Scented blossom on the bough
Means spring is here to stay.

Mary P Linney

The House Of Many Rules

Well it was Sunday afternoon,
Mother went to her mother's,
Not to hide without covers
Father beat us we kept quiet,
Was this to be a riot?
Continued every Sunday
Thank God it wasn't a Monday,
The stairs were very creepy,
My back facing all the fear,
Not for one to hear,
But the house remains in my conscious,
Will my spirit ever leave home?
Not that I would get to Rome,
This home that was destroyed with hate,
My damn mind with all this on my plate,
Grandad got it for us,
Mother had collapsed,
The kitchen was on fire,
If only I had someone to hire,
The black cat smashed
The mirror that never was,
The carpet with many faces,
This wasn't the best of cases,
Walls with many ears,
Full of relief and many tears,
Doors with open minds,
The kind to unwind,
The bedrooms between good and evil,
The bathroom which Father liked to play,
Not the kind for foreplay,
The outhouse for suffocation of death,
The little girl on the road who was killed
Thank God her spirit has been filled,

There is much more inside this little house,
Which is full of love of fear running like a mouse,
Life that will never stop,
Not going back,
It's a good job I didn't go pop,
Is it too late for pain?
At least I hope this doesn't happen again.

Vivienne Anne Thomson

Out In The Sun

It's that time of year
Which costs us dear
Out in the garden
Do beg your pardon
One needs to be seen
Mower to cut grass green
A certain length
Bit more than a tenth
No worries or bother
When using your Hover
As with long pipes
Better in stripes
Poor or rich
Like a cricket pitch
Up and down
Turn around
Back and forth
South to north
It is fun
Out in the sun.

Anthony Higgins

Circles

I'm coming back
To the One that I know.

I don't understand
The things that have been
But I'm coming back
To the One that I know.

And even if
I never know
I pray that You'd still show
In me.

I know I'm known
By You.
So I won't believe the lies
That have clouded my eyes.

I'm coming back
To the One that I know.

Natalie Jagger

Special Needs

Autism, dyslexia, do we understand?
The pain, the suffering, going hand in hand;
Do we meet the cares and needs
Of those for whom it's hard to feed?

Our therapists are trained indeed,
They do their best to meet all needs;
But time and cash are hard to find,
For parents, often, one big grind.

Our SENCOS work through countless hours,
Life for them no bed of flowers;
Psychologists, teachers, parents and the child
All work so hard, at times going wild.

Mum is in the hot seat, most of all,
Living with the problem, always on call;
Unsure of help, unclear where to go,
Reliant on doctor, just wanting to know.

Let's hope that real progress is now under way,
With early reaction and help every day;
With experts and action so early in life,
There's hope and there's prospects to save later strife.

Those early years of action great,
The team approach, it is first rate;
But get the cash to those who count,
Without this cash the problems mount.

John Paulley

Dying In The Rain

You took my heart, you ripped it out
And threw it on the ground.
But you didn't kill it there and then,
You left it there to pound.
I can't believe you would cause me
So much grief and pain.
It seems to me you left our love
With my heart, dying in the rain.

Lyndsey Gill

Sorry World

I would love a world where no drug addicts exist,
Where all children would be missed,
Where children feel safe when they play,
Where children aren't told they're bad, go away.

I would love a world where children are cherished,
Where no one is as selfish,
We have to realise this, we are bringing up the future,
We have to see that it is we who will need looking after,
Why do we need respect when we have none to give?
When are we going to realise it's a sorry world in which we live?

Mary McCulley

So Much Suffering And Pain

How do we pick up the pieces and start all over again,
How can we face another day after so much suffering and pain?

How do we learn to smile again after so much sadness and sorrow,
How do we know things will change and we'll see a
                              brighter tomorrow?

So many innocent people died in such a short length of time,
How did the people responsible think up such a terrible crime?

How do we remember our loved ones who died on that tragic day,
How do we find the culprits, and how do we make them pay?

How do we tell a child where his mother has gone,
How do you tell a father he's lost his beloved son?

How do we say to a lover, yes, his partner is lost,
How on earth can we ever try to count the cost?

Where does this hate all come from, why is it so inbred,
Is it because of religion that so many people are dead?

People are dying from hunger all over the world today,
We must try to help them and feed them, this is the only way.

We must stop all this killing and help them understand
The only way to go forward is peace in every land.

Pauline Mayoh-Wild

Football Tension

It is only a game
Of football, so they say,
But I get so excited,
Don't want my team
To fall, want them to win every day.

While the match is on
I behave so strange,
Some might say I get deranged.
My blood pressure is high,
Feel I'm gonna blow sky high.

I play to death
All my dolphin song CDs,
Try to calm myself down
To the sounds of the sea,
Drink by the gallon camomile tea,
These are the side effects
Of what football does to me.

When I talk on the phone,
Smoking at the same time,
I put my handset in the ashtray,
My cigarette on the telephone line.
I put my TV dinner in the birdcage,
The budgie in the microwave.
All of my symptoms
You can plainly see,
These are the side effects
Of what football does to me.

Ian Barton

The Resident
(Dedicated to Deirdre and Howard - with much love)

There he goes again . . . two shopping bags
A briefcase and an umbrella
I must admit . . . he's a bit of a mysterious fella
He lives beneath us, in the cellar
Never seen anyone go in, never anyone come out.
Perhaps he's mad or a bit 'that way'
Sits and watches clowns all day
Says he sees circuses in his bedroom
In fact he never says much else,
Just keeps 'imself t'imself
Thinks he somehow got left on the shelf.
They say that's the reason why he's a bit 'up here'
Oh dream on, let him dream on
Of slight young divas in sequins and pearls
What must he do to get the girl?
All the thrills of the circus world
He's invited me many a time to come 'share the experience'
This secret life of mine . . .
And I think in a way he was so utterly sardonic
A gloomy clown, who often felt down
Striking camp and moving town.
Oops, there he goes again in his top hat and tails
The lights of the big top allure.
I wished I had his imagination, or is it mine, purely the lack of it . . .
By night he's the king, but in the morning, on his way to work
He is only the 'resident'.
Sans briefcase,
Sans umbrella,
Sans Financial Times,
Sans sanity . . .

Sally Wyatt

Destiny

Tomorrow's like today,
We all pay.
Yesterday is like next week
In the destinies we seek.

Together we make the world one,
Together we can bring peace to everyone.
Apart we cannot exist,
Apart about the conflict we could write a list.

This evening is like the morning,
The sun is dawning,
The moon appearing,
This is the circle of everlasting eternity
The world at harmony.

The stars are like the clouds,
Night and day
Are a part of the universe,
Together, not apart,
Make us who we are today.

Camilla Davidge (14)

Memories

By the river I lazed away
As I passed the time of day;
The water flowed on past me
While making its way to the sea.

I sat and watched the water flow,
All on my own, nowhere to go.
I thought of the good times I had
Playing by this river when a lad.

Here by the river with Mam and Dad,
What great times we all had;
All of us would join in play
On those long, hot summer days.

Along its bank we would dash,
Then jump in and make a splash.
After all the swimming and the fun
We'd lay on its bank in the sun.

What great times we had in the past;
Here in my mind they'll always last.
With my friends and mam and dad,
Here by the river when a lad.

Francis Allen

Battlefield 1914-18

If I can think as clearly
as far and then as deep
to vast churned and
muddy battlefield
of old and always keep
a remembrance of,
and pay homage to
those there maimed
and slain and regret
the decision to inflict
such horror on victims
let us never forget.

Kevan Beach

Growing Up

River Usk you River Usk
Spring from the Brecons deep
Within that mountain's ancient rock
Your lifeblood's waters seep

Downward ever downward
Throughout the heart of Gwent
In mystic mad meandering
Your childhood miles are spent

Playing with the rapids
Your waters mischief white
Sending flapping stilted herons
Aloft in awkward flight

Your youth does not prepare you
For adult future shocks
The magic muse deserts you
As you surge through sordid docks

Your sparkle will be extinguished
When you end your journey south
And you taste the waiting kiss of salt
From the Severn's silted mouth.

Hugh Rose

Signs Of Spring

In spring when birds are mating
Sometimes funny sights are seen
Although the flowers look great
The birds do much more than preen.

An apple core on the grass
Soon attracted two starlings,
They squealed and fought for this prize
But blackbird robbed the 'darlings'.

Now a robin calls daily
For his special soft bill seed,
Another one joined my friend,
A fight broke out with three of breed.

Now trees are covered with mist
Of green, then a darker green,
Crocus, daffodil, snowdrops
All make a beautiful scene.

Little lambs are soon playing
Around their woolly mothers,
Yellow chicks and ducks appear,
Grey bunnies and some others.

Edith Buckeridge

Love Is In The Air

Where there is love the heart is light,
Where there is love the day is bright,
Where there is love there is a song
To help when things are going wrong.
Where there is love there is a smile
To make all things seem more worthwhile.

Where there is love there's quiet peace,
A tranquil place where turmoils cease -
Love changes darkness into light
And makes the heart take 'wingless flight'.
Oh, blest are they who walk in love,
They also walk with God above,
For God is love and through love alone
Man finds the joy that the saints have known.

R Vincent

I Fell Out Of The Sky

Your heart grows with space to
give away, space to explore and
space to build new houses.
We do that as one, as a moving
thing to go further and further, to
take your heart's space, knowing as
we do that there is always room
to grow and always the need to do just so.

As we go higher up and leave ground low
down; as we move and see the bigger world,
I come down, dropping like a thrown stone,
Like I don't belong up in the sky.
But I don't care about falling, about
saying grace and letting go. If
I stay silent, everything will still get done,
get gone as I fall and we build new houses
in your growing space just as I fall screaming
out of the sky, just as your heart fills up.

I touched the sky, so would you rather
die laughing
or
live crying?

   Luke Walker

Clairvoyance

I once saw Stokes a while ago
Giving hope to wounded souls,
All those relatives, long dead,
You contacted with your special skill,
And when you yourself felt ill
And died, I tried to contact you
But all I got was cramp
From sitting too long
In a room full of incense.
The lamp went out at three o'clock
When I gave up and thought,
'Well, Doris,
I don't think much of the afterlife.
You must have lied
To make your living
From the dead and lonely.
If only you could say, 'Hello'
I might believe, but no,
You couldn't do it.
And nor can I.
There's nothing in the heavens,
But only sky.'

Mark Follows

Consequence Of War
(A tribute to the men who died in the Russian submarine, 'The Kursk', August 2000)

To meet in death is the ultimate goal
That's where the heart meets with the soul,
Love and fright soar the body and mind
Taking all thoughts away from mankind.

It's knowing when you take that last deep breath
You'll know it's nearing thyself to death,
To feel this gasp will be thy last
The blood races through the heart so fast.

Thoughts of loved ones riddle thy brain,
Loneliness makes thy body drain,
Look up to heaven you feel so alone
Your soul goes to the twilight zone.

The shell where you lie is now your tomb
You died in anguish, your life was doomed,
Your fate was a disastrous mystery
Your lives will go down in history.

Your loved ones will certainly weep and mourn
Why did you die, oh so forlorn,
They'll never forget your loving face
Once we are born, we're a dying race.

Linda Wright

No Place To Belong

I've always felt 'different'
I don't know why,
Where others would laugh
I would cry.
Where others were satisfied - I was not
I've never been happy with my 'lot'.

I'm never understood, that's how I feel
And everything around me seems unreal.
I live in a world apart from the rest
My imagination constantly put to the test.
My outer shell hides this though
And mostly others would never know.

My dream world is my only escape,
When often I feel my sanity at stake.
It's hard always feeling apart from the rest
And I really do my very best
To fit in where I feel I don't belong
Like an opera singer attempting a pop song.

Why can't I find my niche in life?
Why is living such hard strife?
Others seem to jog along well,
What's their secret? Please do tell.
Is it religion? Is it inbred?
Is it that they are willingly led?

The feelings deep inside me are so strong
But I cannot discover where they belong.
They build up and up with no escape,
There is no outlet - no route for them to take.
So they are suppressed - pushed down low
For they have no other place to go.

Lorna Marlow

The Volcano

Like an angry god,
The volcano spits and vomits in rage
Upon the unsuspecting earth.
Threatened life recoils in horror
As gaseous air chokes all in its path.
Volatile and unstable
The earth returns to its primeval state,
Time and life are suspended
As the earth awaits regenisis.

Joan Thompson

Still Forgotten

Needless upsets, thought-filled mind
Trying to recover.
Trying to exterminate
The negativity of a lover.

A lover I will never have
And one who does not love me.
So why did I try to do it?
Was it so someone would notice me?

Because I listened to a voice
Who tried to comfort me.
Telling me to think again
Saying, 'Don't do it, please!'

But as I listened to those words
As only now, I write,
To convey my thoughts and worries
Thank God, now I survived.

Sometimes the strength of love overcomes
Feelings of lust and wanton.
Of something I could never have,
So it's best left now, still forgotten.

Harriet J Kent

New Dawn

Darkness becomes light
With electricity off
Around eight o'clock
On a mid-winter's morning
In my upstairs room.

I am like a pigeon
Having lost its way on my journey
Departed from the main flock
Way out on my own in time and space
Freedom.

By getting lost, I have found Yahweh,
Life, salvation
Who keeps me safe from evil
When among people.

The light is dawning on my life
Happiness is my lot from now on.

Noel Thaddeus Lawler

Roger And Jane Eyes

There's an angel in
The corner and I'm
Sure she smiles at me
There's an angel in
The corner, may be he
And not a she.

There's an angel in the
Corner looking down
And guiding me
Through good, the
Rough, bad,
The rough every day
And I trust forever
This will be.

Roger Brooks

The Miner

The miner did in days gone by
Take a long, long look at the day's sky
As with his mates he entered the cage lift
That took them down pit at the start of the shift
And daylight was lost for eight hours

They poured out the cage into a railcar
That transported them to the coal face afar
Where they dug out the coal with pick and with shovel
Either lying or kneeling or at best just bent double
And daylight was lost for eight hours

Tea breaks and lunch breaks were taken on site
Midst the dust and the heat in subdued light
That came from their lamps with carbide a-burning
Always wary for signs of gas build-up occurring
And daylight was lost for eight hours.

Near the end of their shift it was back on the car
That retraced its track from coal face afar
Back into the cage and lift out of the mine
Everyone looking upwards for their first sign
That daylight was again theirs.

Archie Livingstone

The Brightest Star

When I look at the stars, I think of Him
Who died for His dreams, but had no sin
Whose love was always for all of mankind
Especially the poor, the sick and the blind.

Our Saviour had a face that showed His love and His trust
He spoke from His heart, in the heat and the dust
One day He was tired and He sat down to rest
And a woman washed His feet and forever was blest.

In the world of today, some things are the same
We weep for our Saviour, His cross and His pain
But His glory lives forever and the day will surely come
When all over the world, He is God's Sacred Son.

Albert Brindle

Sandy

We have a cat called Sandy,
She's anything but male,
She's ginger-striped along her back
And white-tipped on her tail.
We found her in the pouring rain
Some seven years ago;
We took her in and dried her out,
Expecting her to go.
But Sandy had her own ideas,
She liked our nice warm house
And didn't see why she should leave
And have to hunt a mouse.
'We don't want another cat,'
We said. 'They're such a tie,'
But Sandy turned on all her charm
And looked us in the eye.
She wormed her way into our hearts
And got herself a name,
And now she's mistress of the house
And plays her little game.
She knows the warmest places
And where to find the sun,
She knows which are the softest beds
And tries them one by one
She can leap onto a window sill
Without the slightest pause
And even to the mantelpiece
To make her evening tours.

She hardly eats, she scarcely drinks
But she is full of vim
And when the neighbour's tom comes round
She soon dispatches him.
And she will go, like all pets go, and we'll be really sad;
But to have known this funny creature
Will always make us glad.

D A Calow

Spring

Snowdrops bravely bare their heads
In the frozen flower beds.
Then the golden heralds sing
The vibrant trumpeters of spring.

Music from a thousand bills
Is one of Nature's greatest thrills.
Calling birds and cooing doves
Attracting mates with songs of love.

Calves and foals kick up their heels,
Lambkins frolic in the fields.
Nature clothes the rustic scene
In pastel shades of verdant green.

Doreen Hanley

9 Months Old: The Visit

The water from the sky has stopped. Hooray!
Hey! Hullo world! We're out and on our way!
My pushchair slithers, bumps around and jars
Splash, lovely splash and splut along the street,
Across the pavement, past some whiffy cars,
The lift door opens, whose are all these feet?
Clank, swish and jerk and suddenly we're there –
So many faces! Aunt with curly hair
Is playing hide-and-seek behind the door;
'Now I see you, now I don't'
Yes please, go on, go on, I want some more!
Mother takes my coat off - ouch, these sleeves -
Turns up the trousers of my babygro . . .
Oh, what an *interesting* chair I've found,
I'll just reach through and pull the red cloth, so . . .
Hey, what a lovely noise, such an *exciting* sound!
(There seem to be some teacups on the ground).
Mother is walking me towards my toys
My legs are wobbly but she's holding tight.
Ah, good; my rattle with the chewy rings,
My yellow clown is sitting on the right;
Here is my caterpillar with the purple tail,
My green-wheeled toy cart and my squeaky snail.
In fact, it's not bad here, I'll just sit down
And play a bit, it's really quite like home.
I wonder how the service is round here?
Do aunts know just what's what? Will dinner come?
Ah! Here comes Mother with my bib, then all the crew,
Now this deserves a smile or maybe two!
The food smells good, it's in my special bowl . . .
No need to fret, I'm in complete control!

Frances Searle

Monumental

Over there and beyond lies France,
Where peace comes, where peace goes,
To those that have gone before,
Death have taken courage, death have taken bravery,

And death have taken heroes,
In purpose, in brotherhood,
In strength and friendship,
In the grim business of death,

Death does not escape those that fear,
Monumental is the lonely siege,
Where silence is decay upon the wind,
Grey shadows of winter fall upon the corpse.

Melancholy in action under fire,
Where bright red poppies run,
This the charity of men,
Will love conquer war where those that perish?

Where cold steel is run though an enemy shield,
Where great guns roar in triumph,
Deafening men with shrapnel and gas,
Now defying the human spirit in blast.

In freedom and democracy men cry out
Chilling the heart in the explosion,
Barbed wire is a field of blood,
To the mighty unknown soldier, death is thy friend.

Victory is but a medal in reputation,
Requiem, we haven't forgotten the souls of the dead,
Shivering in winter's solemn road,
As each man scribbles a poem of love.

The battle has taken millions in sadness,
Monumental is the lonely siege.

James S Cameron

Enjoying A Pint

Sip awhile the balmy ale
Froth tipped with joyous mirth.
Let convivial prattle wit
The rumble at your girth.

Whence comes the frolic to the mind
Let speech unleashed be,
For harnessed speech be not the speech
That speaks with liberty.

Join the companion who lifts the glass
As his conjured words regale,
Let your elbow rise and fall
At the telling of his tale.

And when the evening touches ebb,
And the watered hop stuns its flow,
Bid them all a goodly night
And out in the darkness go . . . go . . . go . . .

Elwyn Johnso Gorslas

The Black Stallion

As the black mist sweeps through the fields at night
a scream will always follow.
Louder and louder and harder and harder,
your heart will begin to race!
Then the once told story of a man and his horse
seeps through you then you know.
A black cloud approaches you,
as you reach out to touch this cloud you look into one's eye,
as cold as ice, as clear as day,
as free as you ever felt.
You climb up onto the black stallion
and disappear into the night.

Charlene Soan

Journey Into Night

The rolling hills of sadness seemed to dominate the day,
Steadfastly proclaiming that they had come to stay;
The snow-capped mountains of happiness seemed so far away,
Their vision lost in the gathering mist where all seemed dark
and grey.

The gloom relentlessly descended until they had lost their way,
The lanes grew ever narrower in a state of sad decay;
The trees hung like silent witnesses in somnolent array,
Weariness became ever more a force that held them in its sway.

Night came down upon them with a blackness that had nothing
to say,
The cold enveloped them with a force they could not hold at bay;
Eeriness was all about them with a power that made them pray,
Death stalked them until they fell in disarray.

Then the light embraced them and took their spirits away,
Even as their bodies fell and upon the good earth lay;
Evil had entrapped them and treated them like clay,
Goodness still saved them with a majesty all must obey.

J Walker

Unearthed Roots

How did these bones come to rest here?
These bones, carved and fleshed many miles away.
How did this body drift eastwards over the years?
Until finally laying down here, when life's work was done,
In the dignified quiet of this west Suffolk churchyard.
What destiny took your hand and led you here?
All the diggings of genealogy cannot explain your life's course.
Whilst I stand here, wilting flowers fading in hand,
Eyes tracing the letters of your name and dates engraved in stone,
All I can wonder is quite understandable, really.
How did these bones come to rest here?

Leonie Smith

The Awakening

The ravages of winter now disappear
The world awakens to the calm of spring
Trees whisper from their deep sleep
To herald the dawn of life reborn
Love is in the air for all living things
Murmuring, in expressions of love
So beautiful to see, in a restless world
Sample the simple things of life
To kneel, and wait for the beauty of the dawn
To bring the love, and peace, of a new day
And appreciate the awakening of life itself.

Emily Mayor

A Loving Enemy

He loved this country, meant
No harm: send ships to shell
Norway? Corfu? No less
Likely: never forget,
We declared war. The rest -
Oh dear - he never set
Men Herod's work: they left
With notions in their heads
Which stung them wild, misled
By their own bogeymen.

He loved peace - would have kept
It, too: think why he met
The Tsar at Björkö. When
(As ever) pushed, he fell
To war - all their intent,
Not his. Take words for depth,
Misunderstand: his ebbed,
Flowed. Why long stay, unless
He loved this country next?

He loved this country, felt
More English than he said
Later, sure to resent
Our propaganda, threats
Of death. Still, his request,
The chilly day he fled
Into bleak exile: then,
Please, English tea! Still read
English books too, poor wretch,
Poor Kaiser! Mourn him yet.

(NB An old meaning of 'wretch' is outcast/exile)

Veronica M Brown

999

I am looking for a telephone
Or an almanac to the past
There is a number printed somewhere
A direct line of lineage
To the centre of my heart
The numbered suns and countless stars
Fleeing fleetingly apart
Can only come back to the start
And start again, from the start

The circumference a banded space
Where Eros stands in disgrace
The violet sellers, posy peddlers round his girth
Full of piccalilli Piccadilly's mirth
And cockney rhymes
To float across a bustling bus
They call a number nine
A trembling treble emergency
That I want to make you mine
But I'll have to give it time.

Pluto

My Concept Of God

Hark, the Psalmist intones – 'The fool has said there is no *God*,
For, if *He* exists, perceptible would *He* be, my *Lord.*'
If man be of God's likeness, God must be of human stature,
Yet, He's without dimension, invisible, sans feature;
Notwithstanding, Heaven and Earth proclaim His firm existence,
Manifested in Nature's phenomenal transcendence;
There, certainly must be a connoisseur masterminding,
Cosmos' immaculate, perpetual, metrical functioning;
An architect, hallmarked by His intangible attributes -
Of omnipotence, omnipresence, intrinsic virtues -
All beyond the realm of finite human comprehension;
A *Supremo* evolves by *spiritual* integration.
God is the quintessence of all Nature - personified:
Nature begot God, who begot Nature, and energised;
In time, 'Spirit-God' manifested himself physically,
Through Christ who claimed God, the Father and He are One only -
That those who have seen Him, have seen 'Spirit-God', the Father,
The ascending heaven, He and the Father are together,
Reigning in unison till His next mundane arrival;
So God - disembodied Spirit, Nature Personified, is Immanuel!

Welch Jeyaraj Balasingam

Missing You Is Good . . .

Do I ignore my cat as he sits on the mat
Because I miss you?
Do I make a treat I just can't eat
Because I miss you?
Do I start in fear, do I shed a tear
Because I miss you?
Do I contemplate my lonely state
Because I miss you?
Do I watch the clock: tick-tock, tick-tock
Pining for you?

If grass is green and sky is blue
Then yes, yes, *yes*, I do miss you.

But surely missing you is good . . .
It's only natural that I would.
You touch my soul, you make me whole
And when you're near it's very clear
My heart smiles deep within me.

So if it didn't wound my heart
When we are forced apart,
It simply couldn't be
That you're the only he
Whose soul now rests in me.

So can you see, is it *understood*
That missing you is *good?*

Sharon Mary Birch

Life Upon Earth

Erstwhile aloft the warming sun
Has her benevolent work begun,
Streaming life in bright array
'Come be joyful,' she seems to say.
'I'll gladden your heart, lift up awhile,
Banishing gloom by the warmth of my smile.
Dancing and dappling the earth below,
My radiant rays I send you to show
That in the glow of a heaven-sent kiss,
Nothing today will go amiss.
Simply learn to look and feel and trust,
God's love for you is a sun-filled must.
Bringing healing and wholeness, life and scope
All within range as we ask and hope.
Sunbeams dazzling, a promise glowing,
All that is good is glimpsed a-showing.
Parting dark clouds, driving away
I'll bless your life upon earth today.
To show exceeding beauty, for this I strive,
Live for the day and you'll be glad you're alive.
Each moment treasured, precious memories will bring
A purpose to living in Eternity's full spring.
Sun-filled, delighted, loved and caressed,
Yourself in safe keeping, by God's grace blessed.'

Sue O'Donnell

The Dawn Is Yours

There's light in the sky,
The stars are fading away,
Let the dawn be yours
To start a new day.

Dawn has come, awake from your sleep.
Go out in the world, your promises keep.
Fail not in your task, just go on your way,
The dawn is yours, to start a new day.

Yesterday you were sad, but not anymore,
A new day is born, now have a brave heart.
Keep going onwards, your eyes to the fore,
The dawn is yours to make a new start.

The sun is climbing the sky,
Let your hopes climb with it too,
You lost yesterday, today you can win,
Decide this you will do,
Let the dawn be yours, to start a new day.

The day grows warmer
As the cold of night goes away.
Now is the time to build a new way,
For the dawn is yours to start a new day.

C C Strangman

The Spring

A new beginning,
The end over,
The beginning was far away, here.
Precise the way the sun shone,
On you whom beheld it.
The sky, the sun yellow,
The way so plain to see.
Although it's over.
The way to see the being is one with you
Or in another guise, the Devil.
You remember the way you were during the end
For only he would
Rejoice over the end of mankind.
The Devil's pleasure it is the way to
A kingdom lost in a spell,
At any cost.
The way known to you alone.
The way so easy to access.
The devil, the evil one, the alternative judge
Of mankind.
The knowledge that God cannot
Prevent your will and living
In Him you know the best
Way to test yourself is to
Know Him best, to care less about
Yourself is the way to purity and
The triumph is yours even though you've sinned.

Martyn Wheeler

What Are You?

Oh little plant what are you?
I sit and watch you grow,
I know you come from Holland,
But what you are, I just don't know.
You are doing well, you're thriving,
In fact you've grown quite tall;
But when it comes to flowering,
You may not flower at all.
You look more like a Bonsai
As your leaves are so petite.
Your stems are thin and fragile
And yet you grow so neat.
No pruning here is necessary,
You are a tidy little plant,
Your colour is magnificent,
Though to the left you slant.
I am sure you'll just get stronger,
I have every faith in you.
You will live for years and years, I know,
Flower not, or flower do.

   Janette

The Gypsy Fire ~
The Story Of A Painting

See how the logs do burn
And the bracken and the fern
As the fire does blaze
In the evening haze.

See how the gypsy stands by the fire
As the smoke curls higher and higher
The flames give out a lovely heat
As on rising the wind it does meet.

The fire does crackle merrily away
And beside it the gypsy lass does stay
At the end of the day the fire is lit
To await some hours of gypsy bliss.

B C Rice

Silence Of The Lips

Silence of the lips
No word spoken at all
The silence of the lips
Like thunder of heaven roar

What inferno, hate, passion
Love speak
The silence of the lips?

What is the word, not spoken at all?
By a passing smile?
And the silence of the lips?

No words are needed
Speak the silence of the lips
Now a song, the silence is broken
It is a song of love
By a bird on a twig

But the silence of the lips
Never did speak
It is not spoken in English
Or German, or French
The silence of the lips
Now once more again
Talk loud and clear
Black in poetry
Speak softly the silence of the lips
Over and over again.

   Lorand Tabith

Saffron's Garden

Beyond the rustic, rusty doors,
Beneath the moss-turned slabs,
Behind the foliage, browning dead,
The age-old mystery lies.

Once home to bright and sunny days
And careful-tended beds,
Now through the whispering branches bare,
Saffron's secret threads.

Through the bracken, old and dry,
And through the smoggy grey,
Through the cold, the memory steals,
Of her laughter, soft and gay.

Laughing eyes and smiling mouth,
The merriment of the young.
There it is, in the broken stone,
The hook from which she hung.

And now her smiles are locked away,
Stolen by death, the songs she sang.
The mystery, the horror pinned
On the hook from which she hung.

Emily Kitchin

The Future

What does the future hold for this place, this earth?
For our mother who gave us birth
Will we continue to cause her trouble and strife
By showing callous disregard for our fellow siblings' life?
What great possibilities the future could hold
Perhaps a cure for the common cold

Or will we continue with GM foods and our experiments on sheep?
These are the nightmares that wake me from my sleep
Will we continue to cause her pain
By showering her fragile body with acid rain?
Will there be a future, a new day dawning
Before all is destroyed by global warming?

Dumped for trash, a newborn baby utters a piercing cry
Another year, another million of starvation will die
I watch ashamed, in silence, with a melancholy heart
As like savages we continue to tear ourselves apart
I recall the pages of history the same lessons I do see
Of war, prejudice, hatred and fear or death to you and me

Will we ever learn to value the gift of creation
Or will we continue to rape Mother Earth for our own recreation?
Will we ever dare to go where no man has gone before
A place of love and peace, not of hate and war?
Will vain men continue to fight over territory and power
To bathe victorious in the madness of their golden hour?

Will the rivers run red with blood as in ancient times?
Will the evil perpetrators ever pay for their crimes?
Like a plague of locusts we are destroying these rich lands
Holding the future of all mankind in primitive unworthy hands
And sometimes in the darkness when Mother Earth trembles
and quakes
It is no other than a plea as her heart gently breaks.

Denise Startin

147

Running Away

Off on the road again,
With a song on your lips:
Running on, running on empty,
Till the candle burns out.

Running away from home.
Fifteen, so young and yet so old.
Packed your bags this morning
And slid out of the house,
Running away.

Leaving them behind,
The pain and the old struggles,
The arguments and never-drying tears,
Running away.

From being unloved and unwanted,
From being hurt and abused,
From being the only one to see,
It's not the way
Life's meant to be.

Running away,
Not for the first time.
Running away,
Not for the last time.

Child of the sixties,
Heart in revolution,
Get a joint on the way,
Hooked on self-destruction,
Running away.

Full of reformations
And psychedelic dreams,
Dying to change the world
Bursting out into screams,
Running away.

From love and passion,
From kindness and compassion,
From bliss and happiness,
Never looking back.

Seventy-five, so old and yet so young.
Packed your bags this morning
And slid out of the house,
Running away.

Leaving them behind
The ruins of your life,
Spent
Running away.

Lydia Berton

Journeying Alone

I often think about you
As I travel on life's way,
But the journey isn't half as happy now,
We shared so much together
And the skies were rarely grey,
Now the sun has lost a little warmth somehow,
The days grow even longer,
The nights are darker too,
I see the stars but they no longer shine,
Life's road is laid before me,
But the signposts are so few,
The journey's hard, without your hand in mind.

T O Brookes

Old-Style Englishman

In the reign of Victoria he was born;
Adolescent in Edwardian time.
Few years later wounded and battle-worn
In World War One trenches in mud and grime.

Bitterness and revenge did not occur,
Just sadness for losing his fallen friends.
Hoping that carnages would never recur
And governments would work towards those ends.

Old-style Englishman, his word was his bond;
Overseas he spent the rest of his days.
For his king and vast British Empire
He unceasingly worked to gain much praise.

He was a kind man, strict but fair.
A generous, chivalrous Galahad,
Romantic altruist without compare.
Long departed; he was, of course, my dad.

William Barnard

Untitled

Can you see the nightingale
Up there in the tree?
Listen to its trilling song.

The rose is about to burst
Into white blossom.
Its perfume will scent the air.

The seashells sing a song of
Neptune's crashing waves.
Now the tide will be turning.

I heard the voice of Zeus
From his mountain top.
'Don't park on that line!' he said.

Marian Rutland

Garden Beings

Little ladybird
Gobbling garden's aphids
As it marches by

Slippery brown slug
Leaving a slimy trail
Through the cabbage patch

Busy buzzing bee
Pollinating tomorrows'
Red autumn apples

Karina Dingerkus

Untitled

Time ticks by, we cannot sop
this life of ours, forever changing seasons
blending into the life beyond of infinite peace

We are but borrowers in
this life, our time begins at the opening
of our death into the next universe

Eternity watches over us while
we sleep, one breath and we are
as one together in time.

Carol List

A Sleeping Titania

Her incandescent form
Holds an aura
Against malevolent
Creatures of the night
As she awaits
Oberon's regal tender touch.

Paul Wilkins

Summer

Summer is
To shining mathematicians
An additional beam.

Pile heap on heap
My withered garden detritus
Presaging the fall.

Grahame Godsmark

Talking Heads

One finger brushes my hand
as if wanting me to understand
all your eyes long to convey
though you dare not look
up from your book . . .
as your lips half shape
what they will not say
because you've not yet
learned the words for
feelings gay

I let my leg press yours,
feel scalding tremors
pulse through our bodies
like an electric shock . . .
yet you will not look
up at me but lick your lips
nervously, swallowing
the taste of me, coming to
terms with an enduring
curiosity

I let my gaze caress your face,
on sensual mouth place
a gentle kiss, full lips parting
to let my tongue explore . . .
not reading any more (if you
ever were). Though heads, noses,
ears, rush us from all sides
like attitudes . . . keep fiddling
with that shirt button, it's
a lifeline

Together, against
the Hydra.

R N Taber

Margarita

My first love was a gipsy girl
Who lived in a caravan.
Her name was Margarita,
And she came from a famous clan.

She dressed in vivid reds and golds -
Wore sequins in her hair,
Her laugh was tinkling silver bells,
And her smile was, oh, so rare.

We played throughout the summer long,
In happy, carefree ways,
And childish innocence and bliss
Filled all those wondrous days.

And then one day I came to call
And the caravan had gone;
And never in my life since then
Have I felt so forlorn.

She did not wait to say goodbye -
She couldn't bear the pain;
She knew it was unlikely
That we would meet again.

And though so many years have passed
Since we were forced to part,
Some love for Margarita
Still lingers in my heart.

    ACIS

First Love

You meet me on a bus, in a cafe or lane,
You know that it's love, it feels like a pain.
She may be curvaceous, vivacious or plain,
But you know that it's love, you walk in the rain.

You can't sleep or think, you can't eat or drink,
Your mind's in a whirl, all flowers are pink!
You know that it's love, you know there's a link.
You know that young lady's brought to the brink.

Her smile and her touch, the feel of her hair,
Makes your heart miss a beat, when she tells you she cares.
Walks over hills, the dales and the byways,
Ecstasy as you walk love's highways.

You wonder why God gave you all this,
A squeeze of the hand, a cuddle and kiss.
You feel it can't last, love is sublime;
You can't sleep a wink until you see her next time.

Your pulse races madly, as she gives you a smile,
You look for your love nest, a gate, or a stile.
Your arms round each other, you tenderly kiss,
Both lost to the world in that moment of bliss.

You gently unwind, and walk to your bus,
And think to yourself, 'The world envies us.'
In time you may marry, you may of course part,
But you know that old feeling is still in your heart.

You thank God he gave you that very first love,
And the gift of remembrance, sent from above.

Lionel J Nokes

In This Garden

In this garden I feel safe
Amongst the majestic trees
So solid and dependable
The leaves speak to me
And flowers smile upon me.

I came here for comfort
For no particular reason
Just because I felt I needed
Something to enfold me.

The plants mingle in drifts of colour
To captivate the eye
And the butterflies dance among them
The kind sun warms me
And makes me feel loved again.

I close my eyes
And hear the crows gathering overhead
But even this does not disturb my tranquillity
I have found the peace I was seeking
And feel loved in this garden.

Fiona Franklin

Grant Me Love

My love for you is so imperfect,
It feels as though the heat of the day,
Shall cause it to wither away.
The only way I know to make it grow,
Is to love you all the more.
If I say a word unkind,
Through reckless and selfish thinking,
Water me with loving patience,
Until I am refreshed.
If I argue with sinful pride,
Nourish me with simple kindness,
So there's no room left
In my heart for madness.
If I fail to be tender or understanding,
Hold my hand
So that I may feel your warmth.
Above all, share with me
The sunlight of your smile.
For in all these things,
A man's spirit cannot help but grow,
And in all eventuality,
All tears of the heart
Shall be wiped away.
Showing in time and season
A more perfect love.

Ronald D Lush

Their Angel Eyes

Their angel eyes sparkle brighter
Than the stars at night
Their bright angel smiles
Are always warm and wide
And softer than the snow
On the wide open countryside
Their soft angels' lips are sweeter
Far sweeter than honey to kiss
And their slender angel bodies
Feel so warm and tender
In my arms
Every time I hold them both
Closer and closer
To lucky old me

Then every night as I hold them both
Tenderly but tight
I thank the good Lord above
For letting me know
And for feeling the love
Of the two very sweet and beautiful angels
In my life
One my beautiful daughter
The other my sweet angel wife
Who are both called Linda Marie

   Donald John Tye

My Girl

There she was,
Standing on the street.
When my eyes fell on her,
She swept me off my feet.

Someone so beautiful,
I'd never seen before.
I stood there staring,
Till my heart got sore.

I plucked up the courage,
To ask to take her out.
This girl is meant for me
I knew without a doubt.

I tore out my heart,
And put it in her hand.
And then I replaced it,
With a gold wedding band.

Now she has left me,
And torn me apart.
But I'll sit here waiting,
As she still has my heart.

Rachel I love you,
And will to the end.
The rest of my life,
With you I will spend.

Nigel Quinn

Running True

We chat for a while
and walk apace
while fluffy bits start
to gather, wipe the
sweet smile from
heaven's face;
Pause under a willow's
weepy awning, ponder
killing off a desperate
yearning for each other
on the spot - but
cannot;
Such tears for the death
of innocence, falling
like spring rain!
Like a river, blood
running faster
in the vein;
Storm warning false,
heaven at ease with
the day again;
Fluffy bits on the river
like wreaths, floating
in the sun;
Snug inside the willow,
your heart for
a pillow;
Feted by a lark, giving
nature's belated
blessing.

Spring days, running
true - for gays too.

R N Taber

Charlie

I picked her up, for our very first date,
Her mother said, 'Rosie, now don't you be late.'
'It's alright Mum, we're not going far,
And anyway, John has got an old car.'

We went to the pictures and sat at the rear,
I fancied my chances, as it would appear.
The film was called Bambi, exciting, I know,
But remember it was, a long time ago.

I put my arm round her in case she was scared,
She nestled towards me, it seemed that she cared.
We kissed and canoodled through most of the show,
But just as it finished and we started to go,
I stared in amazement, was I going mad,
For three rows in front sat the rear of her dad.

We all stood for 'God Save The Queen' in those days,
After which he turned round with a look that amazed,
It wasn't a smile, more a glare and a huff,
I waved sheepishly to him, it wasn't enough.

We hurried off quickly along with the crowd,
And Rosie was looking more nervous than proud.
We reached my old banger, so cold and iced up,
But it wouldn't start, it was just my bad luck.

Her father had walked home in just half an hour,
But when we arrived after midnight, he glowered.
'I suppose that old banger broke down,' is what he said,
I nodded politely and went home to bed.

   John Cook

Thank You God For 60 Years
(9.3.1942 ~ 9.3.2002)

Through all these sixty diamond years
we've had our laughs and shed our tears;
in troubled peace and World War Two
was where Love blossomed, where Love grew;
a time when life was 'Bitter Sweet'
with Army leave our chance to meet;
a time when war kept us apart,
a testing time for mind and heart;
a time to thank the God above
who kept us on the path of Love
until the days of peace came round
when in our babes great joy we found.
So as we reach the Diamond Day
there's just these words I wish to say
to Joan, my Winifred, my wife
who's shared the ups and downs of life,
who's put up with my absent mind
and habits of the strangest kind,
who's longed for glamour and romance
(instead of which she's ironed my pants):
As all these years have swiftly flown,
I hope her heart has always known
I'll love her till the cows come home!

Tony Lomas

My Love

On the darkest day
I think of you and a light
Shines bright in my heart.
The day I met you
I knew we were meant to be
A voice within told me
We're never going to be apart.

Emma Winn

When Two Hearts Run Dry

I remember so vividly
The day . . .
The hour even
The corridor at school
When I first saw her and
What she wore and smelt like
She sucked out my breath
And pumped my heart with a strange, new emotion
Never felt before
My stomach was a vacuum
Yet my heart overflowed with four star love
As we experienced our first, silent tryst
Our first, breathless, awkward, numbing kiss
I heard only the blood rushing in my ears
And our sexual awakening
More potent than any cider
With any Rosie
Under any hayrick
But through time we forgot to check the dial
That read
Running on empty
No place for a refill
There is no filling station of love
When two hearts run dry.

Ian Speirs

Shadow-Play

Your face I saw.
Beneath a beard.
A closely interwoven or tangled mass.
An unreal thing.
The time of a wink,
The hairy arch above the eye.
A glass to assist the sight
Resembling spectacles.
A well-marked character.
Wearing an old, green anorak,
material of various types and thicknesses.
At the end of the day
to make weary.
Attending like a shadow.
To direct glancingly.
Standing opposite to.
Looking towards . . .
could I speak
eyes meet,
paradise.

Pat Jones

That First Kiss

That first passionate kiss, I must get it right,
Do I just hang loose or squeeze her up tight
I feel like a youngster in the first flush of youth
Will it be on the doorstep or in the corner phone booth?
A peck on the cheek, a mother's goodnight kiss
Like a real movie star! Oh how I wish
Perhaps the heavens will open and I'll be on cloud number nine
Will the earth move and I will feel in my prime
Oh heck, let's go for it, she knows who I am
There she is, too late, she's pushing a pram.

Trevor Beach

Who'd Have Thought

Who'd have thought
On that bright excursion day
That the wine of rich wit
Would turn to such gall.

Who'd have thought
That those roses of May
Which such tenderness brought
Would stink with a foul decay.

Who'd have thought
That a spring so fresh
Would breed a love so false.

But who could have thought
That come the following June
Each danced to a new tune
And forgotten was that last waltz.

Mary Frances Mooney

Holding Hands

Your hand touched mine
I could feel the warmth,
As you smiled at me
You picked the biggest, white rose
I had ever seen,
Holding hands you gave to me.
We sat and talked
All the while I looked beyond your smile.
Then I felt a chill,
You were no longer there
Just a memory in the cool, night air.

Laura Sorrell

A Poem Of Love(s)

It was natural for him to love her
And to tell her so
With words from hidden agenda,
To hear, to read, to know.

It is not the love of adolescence
Of finding, of fumbling, of sex,
Nor excitement of newly-found pleasures
No knowledge of true love as yet.

It is neither the love of first manhood
Of change, experiment, delight,
Such love is not often lasting
Too many give up the fight.

It is neither the love of those middle years
When experience of life should provide
A wonderful, unselfish, sexual love,
Of happiness none can deride.

It is neither love found in retirement
As passion subsides through the years,
With a smile on the lips of remembering
Such kindness, such patience, no tears.

It is though a love without passion,
A love that true friendship can bring,
A love contained in walled gardens,
An everlasting, 'many-spendored thing'.

Stan Dwight

My Child

Today, I had a thought,
A bright thought you see,
Today I thought of you,
And what you mean to me,
You're full of sunshine, hope and joy,
In fact, you're such a special boy,
With big, brown eyes and cheesy grin,
Short, dark hair and clear, fresh skin,
You make me laugh and sometimes cry,
But you're the reason I survive,
You are my life, my dream come true,
You are my child and I love you.

Janet Evans

My Peace

Time . . .
Peace . . .
Cutting the grass back
And watching it grow with ease,
Complete peace of mind
I'm not worried about time.
My peace . . .
Waking up
Next to you
Feeling you there
Before I awake,
Feeling the warmth
Knowing that you're on your way
That it won't be long,
Wrapped around each other's fingers
As delicate as these smoke trails
As strong as the last clinch or touch
Before sleep.
You are my soul love
My foreseeable future
My faith and thoughts, an angel for an atheist
My best friend
Two halves of the same brain
My peace of mind
My peace.

Kevin Rolfe

Timeless

If there wasn't any time,
I'd never have to leave.
We could hold each other
by the hand,
for eternity.

We'd always be together here,
have no other worries.
I'd gave into your blue eyes
and hold you
even tighter.

There'd be no day, and no night,
but we wouldn't care.
Because time has no meaning
when we're
here alone.

J Webb

Idyllic Love

There is a finely, painted eye miniature,
That stares at the viewer,
Portraying a magical charm, from its art;
And encased are two locks of silken hair,
Entwined in a locket for love's heart,
Yet romance casts such a spell of emotion,
When kindled eyes, look full of love and devotion.
And yet with fresh spring comes the springtime flowers,
And primrose, violet and bluebell bowers,
Fleeting weeks of ever-changing hue,
Such romantic weeks for love that is true.
And enchanting days, and the realm where Cupid flies,
Through spellbinding hours that will immortalise,
Always enkindling loves spirit, within the begotten dream,
Bewitching two hearts, with love's breath that is between.

Christine Hare

Legacy Of Love
(Dedicated to Shirley, with my love)

Another springtime, another April, another 29th May,
When our spirits unite as one, in loving memory today.
Different women, and sisters born of the same mother,
Our first thoughts this morning will turn to each other,
Knowing what each will carry silently within,
Whatever our different day for us colours in . . .
Sombre blackness and the fears of night,
Softened with hope at dawn's breaking light,
As you and I cloaked in past memories,
Get to grip with this day's harsh realities;
Me in the country, you there in town,
Face masks in place reveal neither sadness nor frown.
Each of us with our particular burdens to bear,
Will converge and commune, in thoughts of the mother we shared;
Our personalities, characters, indeed lifestyles, so opposite,
But family bonds forged over long years, make you and I
as close sisters, a complimentary composite.
Our mother's loving, devoted, good and selfless parentage,
Is yours and my unique and wonderful inheritance.
Along with our common blood ties and genes,
She intuitively gave us something extra it seems,
For you and I, although so individual as sisters and daughters,
Bond emotionally together, with our shared element of water,
Understanding each other, despite our differing needs,
With tolerance, compassion, love and deep friendship;
Fruits born from Mona, our dear mother's seeds.
In this landmark year of yours, we shall celebrate with pleasure,
Our memories more than most, because of our happy
                                        childhood together;
So, my sister, as we unite, though apart on this unforgettable day,
Let us strengthen those bonds, in loving gratitude to Mum,
as for her, together we pray.

Annette Harris

Brief Encounter

He stood there staring at me,
as he had been for a while.
His calm and quiet expression
showed a flicker of a smile.
I was not at all alarmed,
but I really must confess,
when it comes to confidence,
I have won no great success.
I said, 'Please stop that staring,
better still just go away.'
He shook his head quite slowly,
not a single word to say.
I showed my agitation
and waved a weapon up high.
Mock horror was his answer,
with a twinkle in his eye.
I watched him for a moment,
his smile got even wider.
Could I be so cruel to such
a loving, little spider?
The nozzle and the vacuum
were pushed out into the hall.
Then he blew a kiss to me
and went off to climb the wall.

Catherine J Clough

Don

He's worked so hard all his life,
His hands they are now suffering,
He and his mates they built the house,
In which we are now living.

We've been together for fifty-two years,
Married for only fifty!
We've also been through thick and thin,
Not much money, but tried to be thrifty.

Trained as a carpenter at Moss's,
This was not his intent,
At the age of fourteen he left school,
To be a bricklayer he was sent.

A very handsome chap he was
When hair was on his head,
And after all these years with him
I still don't know when he's mad.

When I am driving along in the car,
It's though I am just learning,
'Slow down, go on, you change too soon,'
To park, 'Too soon you're turning.'

For all his faults I love him still,
Though he is aggravating,
So often at cross-purposes we speak,
And not really debating.

Mary Armstrong

I Do Remember
(Sandy, Beloved Scottie Dog)

We loved - so loved
The woodland way
River's edge
Along the Tay
Sprite protecting
In our time
Sharing joys
Sandy - yours and mine
Dynamic force
Then held us fast
Destiny whispering
Came to pass
Your eyes of soul
Life's sacred song
I do remember
An eternal bond.

Irene Gunnion

Off

I dreamt of us two being together
But you made it clear
That this won't happen - never
That was my greatest fear.

Your shining eyes, your wonderful smile
I was so happy - for a while.

I dreamt of you saying you love me
You said it
You meant it
But more should it never be.

I love you so
But off you go.

I still hear the words you said,
I still feel your pain.
In my heart regret
Will always remain.

Am remembering you holding me real tight
I only said, 'It's all right.'

My fears -
A future without you,
All my tears
Didn't help, came true.

Is this God's will?
'Cause I love you still.

Perhaps my tears will dry one day,
Maybe I find my way,
But in my heart a pain
Will always remain.

I love you so
But off you go.

Sandra Lemke

The Triumph Of Love

For countless years I searched for you,
But you never came.
Each day, week, month and year
All seemed the same.

And now in the twilight of my years,
You have come to me at last,
My sweet love, my darling, my soulmate,
I have forgotten the past.

Let my song of joy and gladness
Into the heavens fly
And mingle with the angels
To return to you and I.

Blessings of a thousand fold,
Descend to us from above,
And expiate the loneliness,
When I was without my love.

Irene Greenall

Love

Love crowns our lives,
Invisibly enthrones
Guides in adversity,
Permeates our homes.
Embraces bonded in purest gold,
Increase in value as we grow old
Unspoken thoughts then mutually known,
Unsynchronised actions forever outgrown.
At the end of the day how easy to see,
What a gift love's blessing truly can be.

L J Harries

Love Letter

Kept close to my heart
Though tattered and torn
Now, many years old but treasured still
We were young and so in love.
He has gone, leaving me
Bereft and broken hearted.

Irene Brown

My Wife

Gwen was my dearest wife,
She was the light of my life:
I can still see her face,
Suffused with grace.

As I recall our years together
In every kind of weather,
A mixture of laughter and tears,
They are unforgettable years.

We were young when we met,
But our course was set:
Our steps were being guided,
And our future was decided.

As we wended our way,
We enjoyed every day;
Just being together
In every kind of weather.

There were ups and downs,
There were smiles and frowns;
Life was sometimes grim,.
But our love never grew dim.

The years were rolling by
With many a lingering sigh:
For we dreaded the day
When it would all pass away.

But God who gave us our love,
Lives in Heaven above
Where He intends us to spend
Eternity without end.

Kenneth E Jinks

Just A Bit More Than Friends?

Like trees swaying in a summer breeze
A look from you, brings me to my knees.
I'd let you know, how much I care
I've tried in a letter, but wouldn't dare.

My love for you continues to grow
Even if you can't see it though.
It should be obvious; it should be clear;
The fact I love you so much my dear.

When you decide to flirt with other girls,
I can only think that they're such cows.
I can't understand why you don't see,
That I just want you to love me.

You think that we are just good friends,
But the love I have, drives me round the bend.
I always think about you, you're in my head
And in my dreams, when I go to bed.

Anon

True Love

True love is precious and wonderful like a
possession of exquisite beauty.
That is cherished, guarded and valued for
its priceless bounty.

Is this love when my heart goes thumpety-thump and skips a beat?
I feel deliriously happy as we twirl and waltz, cheek to cheek.
We could dance the whole night through
for love rules our hearts and dancing feet.
I cannot hide this new emotion
that suddenly makes me feel complete.
I never, ever dreamed love could be like this,
such sheer, heavenly bliss.
It seems to embrace the very air we breathe
and with God's blessing we are caressed.
My head is high in the clouds and it is so hard to part company
and kiss goodnight.
For I wish to stay forever together under the stars
and the gentle moonlight.
A soft, light breeze wafts enchanting music in the air
that charms and delights my heart.
The night displays its magical powers and we praise God's holy name,
'How wonderful thou art.'
A shooting star flickers and dies, never more will it twinkle
and light the night sky.
For a moment we felt sad.
I wonder would it feel pain as it was thrust downward to Earth?
I wonder why did it have to die?
When a star falls to Earth one must make a wish,
I believe wishes come true.
Do you?

Elizabeth Myra Crellin

Island

I found an island in the night
Where finally I found her.
She lived under a golden light
That ever would surround her.

Brighter than the morning star
Does she appear before me.
She knows I came from very far
And need her to adore me.

We drift within our own lagoon
And play with friendly creatures.
I recognise this silver moon
And praise this omen's features.

Richard Van der Draaij

Love Is In The Air

Deep in the quietness of my mind,
You are there before me, gentle, kind,
Your dark eyes, smiling are forgot never,
Though our last meeting may be far behind.

Sweet memories, cherished, remembered still,
Brief encounters tho' at times they were.
They fill the days with poignant joy,
And not a little does my heart stir.

In some private moment peaceful, serene,
Perhaps you too may yet recall
Those few hours, sweet-talked and close,
When our encircled world meant all.

Lizbeth Cooke

My Very Own First Kiss

During the war, 'twas from Africa that I came,
into a Scottish hospital for the wounded, sick and the lame
For weeks in a haze I lay in my bed
Until the doctor came and said
'I think in this bed you may no longer lay,
there's a concert tonight with Evelyn Laye.'
Accompanied by a lovely nurse,
I was happy, I had no need for a hearse.
With shouts and whistles galore
Evelyn came back and did an encore.
On the way back to my bed, we sauntered,
stopping outside the nurses' quarters.
That nurse gave me a goodnight kiss
my, oh my, that was pure bliss.
That night in my bed I did lay
thanking that singer, Evelyn Laye.
The next morning, that nurse smiled,
'Good morning Arthur,'
I smiled back, *after:-*
60 short years, we have been wed,
It's strange that we met whilst I was in bed.
Yet, I still remember our very first kiss.
Every night, I still have a kiss, yes sir, I never miss.
I love her to bits, until it hurts
Yes, she is still my loveable, kissable nurse.
She has looked after me through thick and thin
without her where would I have been?
As I have said before, I still love her to bits
it's all those years ago, I still remember our very first kiss.

A G Snow

The First Love

What's the first love?
It's great heart's desire,
Great desire, a shoot of fire,
Hot, but magic, so gentle,
Its great tide,
Breaks the heart's obstacle,
Burns the kiss fire,
That unites lovers' desire,
And opens the door of love,
To ecstasy of love,
A tide of love doesn't die,
It continues and remains ever and ever,
Becomes stronger and stronger,
Can't extinguish, never,
But unites the minds to love,
Never kills the desire,
For unity of hearts,
Great ecstasy of lovers.
That's the first love!
Lovers can't forget,
It remains so tight!
Burns the hearts of lovers,
It's the spark of fire, for lovers.

Jalil Kasto

For Mo

Forgive me for
loving you
forgive me for caring
for hoping that you
might also be sharing
the warmth and the
feelings
that I hold for you
so clear, so simple
so honest
so true.

Whatever you wish
that I will do
all that I want
is to be good
for you
to be held in the glow
of what light you
might give
to make that much
easier this life
that I live.

For in all my sorrow
to you I've been true
ask of me what you
will except to stop
loving you
for this above all
I never could do
till the end of my days
I will always love you.

Edward B Evans

Sleep-Dream

You were in my dream last night,
In plush, pink armchairs,
Drinking coffee, or was it tea?
As if we had no cares.

You're not usually in my sleeping dreams,
So why were you there last night?
I spend my daytime wishing I was with you,
My nerve ends all uptight.

I want to sleep-dream of your love
Cos nothing's happening for real;
It would be one way of being in touch
With some sort of relationship-deal.

Those plump armchairs, in pink, if you please!
Must mean something strong,
Some Freudian aspect of the sexual act?
S'funny, it couldn't be more wrong.

We've never ever shared more than a peck
Of a kiss upon your cheek.
You've never attempted to kiss me back,
Though I've hoped from week to week.

My love for you is as deep as the cushions
On a well-upholstered settee,
Not prim and proper, but comfortable, rounded,
Well-padded and warm, like me!

Kate

A Daisy Chain

(Dedicated to Rosy Fox, my special childhood friend)

A yellow and white daisy chain across our hearts,
A country walk, a custard tart, a game of draughts,
A big, brass bed in a tiny, upstairs room,
A love, a friendship, childhood memories bloom.

We giggled and laughed as we jumped the brook,
And moan and groan as the cowpats we had to look
Out for, the long summer days we shared with our dear nan and pop,
St Patrick's Lane and our daily walk to the shop.

Our pretty daisy dresses we wore with such pride,
We thought we were the bee's knees, we just couldn't hide,
Our sheer delight at having the same frocks,
It's just such a shame no one thought to buy us matching socks.

But we didn't mind, we were wrapped in such care,
By a very special couple, a wonderful pair,
We'd run in the sun, sit on the green, a friendship never to part,
Because we sat and built a daisy chain that forever binds our hearts.

Lore Mary McIntyre

One Love Only

One love only there is for me,
Since first I saw you and
Heard you sing. That song
You sang, took my heart away,
One love only, there is for me
And that love is you.

Time came when my love grew dim,
It seemed it was going to fade away,
But when I saw you, once again,
One love only, there was for me
And that love was you.

Other singers, have I seen
Other songs have I heard,
Not one can take your place,
One song only, there is for me,
One love only, there is for me,
And that love is you.

Now you are gone, but your
Song lingers on,
Lingers on in a heart that is sad,
I am longing and hoping to see you again,
One love only, there is for me,
And that love is you.

C C Strangman

You Will See A Stranger . . .

Long years ago, in February, I met her on a train.
I was reading a book, but watching who came
And went. She came and shared a table, sitting opposite.
I offered her a cigarette - and lit it for her.
We talked, as if we'd known each other always
About ourselves; that I was bound for Durham
And an interview; that she went already
To the City University; and both aimed
At an English (Literature) Degree.
We talked of books, and plays, and poets,
And of inconsequential things,
Until the train pulled into Central Station,
Where I stayed in my seat,
And she skipped off towards morning lecture,
Leaving me dazed, amazed, by such a lovely girl.

I went on to Durham, spent a windy night in Castle College,
Attended my interview, and caught the train
Towards my south-west Midlands home, out in the sticks.
Eventually, the train came back to Central Station,
Waited some time, then faced the final 'leg'.
Travel-worn, I dozed . . . and suddenly
She slipped again into the facing seat,
Returning the cigarettes I'd pressed on her before.
'I thought you might be on this train. I didn't search for long.'
We went on talking, talking like old friends.

I told her of my interview, and hopes and doubts.
She told me bits from lectures and her aspirations,
And, all too soon, we reached her local station,
Where she stood up, 'I have enjoyed the trips,'
'Thank you,' she said, and touched my hand, 'Goodbye.'

I watched as she showed her season ticket,
Went briefly from my view, then as she crossed a pool of light
She waved towards the train and me . . .
And suddenly it hit me like a hammer -
We hadn't exchanged addresses, even names . . .

A very, special girl had touched my life,
And gone . . .

Robert T Collins

Together

Together
We can shut out the outside world
Together
We are strong
Together
It doesn't matter what life throws
Because together
We are one.
And if the path should fade away,
If I get lost and sad
Remind me of all the
Wonderful and special times we have
And though sometimes
We're tired
And yes, we bicker too
Remember that
Together
We can always see it through.

Clare King

Lucy's Love

The theme of Lucy's life was kindness, love and care
Her beauty, radiance and warmth circulated everywhere
The love of her family was the love of her life
She was their anchor through life's turmoil, storms and strife
As Lucy told lovely stories of her parents, children and other
                                                  loved ones too
Her wonderful, genuine love and pride came shining through
With treasured family photos around her Lucy was happy
                                                  and content
She counted her many blessings and knew they were heaven sent
Lucy's gentle, appreciative nature was greatly admired by all
She gave thanks for every act and token, no matter how small
Today, she is in a better place at eternal rest with God above
We give thanks for a mother, grandmother and great grandmother
Who was so full of love.

Angela Moore

Just An Elf

Love is in the air
it's all about everywhere.
But the thing is
I just don't care.
My life is as I want it to be
relationships are not for me.
I would rather sit by myself
and get a book down off the shelf.
Saving what I would have spent,
building up my wealth.
But all this is an illusion
if it affects one's mental health.
It has not affected me
but then again I am just an elf.
Don't tell everyone
keep it to yourself.
You might just catch sight of me
in the clearing of a delph.

S Glover

The Golden Years

Congratulations to the many couples,
Who have stood the test of time,
Their marriage worked through thick and thin,
To reach the 'Golden Mile'
They shared their joys on many a day,
Shed lots of tears along the way,
They learned the art of give and take,
Accepted the blame for some mistake,
Good fortune must have smiled on you,
To guide you through your strife,
For yours is a special kind of love,
That's carried you both through life.

Tom Grocott

Quiet Thoughts

One prays that through our time,
That we are able to do what is right.
For temptation is always there,
Keeping off the wrong paths a fight!

So many like to take the easy way out,
For it's easier to go along with the flow.
Having a mind of your own is special
One must remember only man said *No!*

Being honest and true to yourself finds,
The treasures of life are yours for free.
So accept what was rightfully yours and,
Life's love and beauty will flow for Thee!

There is a beautiful person in us all,
So let it shine out for the world to see.
For there was more to life than objects,
There's something special in you and me!

Only those that had eyes that didn't see,
Ears that didn't hear and no communication.
Missed the treasures and mysteries of life,
Hence search in vain for some salvation!

Life is all around us perfectly designed,
So why did man think he had to put it right?
It was as we used our resources that,
Gave us a future and kept happiness in sight!

When one has understood what life is about,
We can thank the Lord and scream and shout!

Ann Beard

First Love

First love, faint love
Growing stronger every day
Won't leave me on my own
It never goes away.

It's been driving me crazy,
Completely up the wall
I think that it's too much for me
I can't take it any more.

First love, faint love
Can't admit it to your face
That I find you super stunning
We should be more than mates.

I don't know how to tell you this,
You're always in my head,
In the day when I'm awake
And at night when I'm in bed.

I don't know what it was,
That made me fall in love with you,
But I know that it's the real thing
And I don't know what to do.

I guess it's not a silly crush
I can't help the way I feel
Do you feel the same as me?
That would make my dreams for real.

Its destinies way of telling me
That it's in a league with fate
And what I'm really trying to say,
Is will you join me on a date?

Gemma King

Untitled

No words could describe
my love for you
The joy I feel with you
by my side.
Knowing you're there for me
lightens each day
As we share our memories
our hopes and our dreams.
Grey clouds are banished
just by your smile,
Blue skies are promised
just by your touch.
Who would have thought
when first we met
The path we had to follow
but I can tell you this my love
it's a path I've joyfully followed.

Z Collisson

The First Kiss ~ That Missed

In the year nineteen hundred and forty-one
I reached the age of fourteen
When I met a young officer in the
Royal Air Force
He teased me, he cuddled me
And promised me my first kiss
But alas, I should have foreseen
There would come the day
When he would be sent away
To a far away Scottish town
So, my first kiss came amiss
Since then much time has blown
With something a fourteen
year old did miss
And that was her very first kiss.

B C Rice

That's The Love In My Heart

The love in my heart is faithful and strong,
If you come and take it, you'll never go wrong,
The love in my hart has been there so long,
The love in my heart beats out a love song.
That's the love in my heart.

The birds in the trees were the love of my life,
But now the love in my heart just yearns for a wife,
That love in my heart, it is there just for you,
It brings out my feelings, for you they're so true.
That's the love in my heart.

Such a beautiful maiden deserves only the best,
So just come over darling and I'll do the rest,
I'm a kind-hearted man, in the prime of my life,
Feeling sure that I have found me, the perfect wife.
That's the love in my heart.

We have spent time together, now my heart just yells,
This is your woman, let us hear those wedding bells,
The love in my heart is faithful and strong,
Now that you've taken it, you'll never go wrong
That's the love in my heart.

Wenn-The-Penn

When I Am With You
(Dedicated to my boyfriend, Graham)

When I am with you, I feel as free as a bird
     in a clear, blue sky.
When I am with you, my problems seem to fade away,
     seem so easy, so useless.
When I am with you, a raging storm is chased away,
     by a sunny day.
When I am with you, I don't need to put on a smile
     it's there when we meet.
When I am with you, a rich sense of love erupts
     inside of me so real and loyal.
When I am with you, it's the best part of my life.

I love you honey with all my heart
Thank you for being there when I needed you most.
I love you always and forever from your little girl.

Sarah Collett

Love Is In The Air

Could this be love, that's in the air?
Now the trees are no longer bare,
The trees now, no longer bare,
Perhaps my feelings I now can share,
A friend he's been since my husband passed away
He's helped me through the wintertime
With phone calls and letters at any time.
His son, also now has passed away
But in his heart he'll always stay
To lose a loved one is very sad,
But, it's brought us closer, and that can't be bad.
We've helped each other through our troubled times,
We are even closer, now we find.
Could this friendship develop more?
As we walk, hand in hand, along the shore.
We talked, of our loved ones, now not around,
As the sea laps against the pebbles,
Our voices and the sea the only sounds,
To share our thoughts and our memories
Could this friendship develop into more?
We will just wait and see
As we stroll along the beach, near the sea!

Janice Jackson

Only Us There

I asked you
For a dance
To a familiar tune
A saxophonist
Gently squeezed notes
From his instrument
The leader
Waved his baton
Looking behind him
At us
Lights
From the giant globe
Sparkled in your hair
The ballroom
Seemed
Empty
Other dances *dancers*
Were invisible
They waltzed through us
There was only
Us there.

Paul Wilkins

A Perfect Match

According to astrology,
Both you and I combine.
For though my element is air
And you're a fire sign,
We are wholly compatible
With many things in common.
You are the classic Aries male
And I the Libran woman
Your birthstone is a diamond
And your ruling planet Mars.
Your favourite colours are red and pink,
You're the head sign of the stars.
My birthstone is an opal
And my ruling planet Venus.
My favourite colours are blue and yellow,
And so you see, between us
We could do so much together,
Without ever getting bored.
For we truly are compatible
And could reap every reward.

Janette Leese

Lost Love

She slips and flickers away
On that bright, summer's day
Memories abound
Whispering grasses lamentation at the sound
Love lost in youth's mire.
Before pain puts on its winter attire
The early morning sun
Indicates hope that daybreak has begun
Feelings of love lost and won
Emotions immersed in reckless pity
Remembering her so young and pretty
But all is wasted passion
Like a fad - like a fashion
It comes from time to time
When the world is light like summer wine.

Finnan Boyle

Detail Worked In Love

Beautiful, beautiful blossom so fine,
Bending the tree in silent spring worship sublime.
A sight full of wonder, of splendour, of awe,
Bare branches bedecked bound in God's law.
Fresh flowers frilled by the work of His hand,
So delicate, so clustered, so pure and
So white, yet tinged at the tips, the cut away edge
With a blush of soft pink, forever a pledge
Of precision, perfection, a painter's fine hue,
A detail worked in love, for me and for you.
The hawthorn blooms in winter, same species in May,
To carry clustered red berries, the family's name 'Rose a Say'.
Autumn's bright harvest, hips and scarlet field haws,
It's glorious to be a free, a fresh out of doors!
God's gift in abundance, a breathtaking sight,
To help us stop, praise and wonder so ever we might
Thank the Father of all things, both great and small,
Seasons for living, endless enjoyment for all.
Fresh flowers for the springtime, sun-kissed they grew,
The Creator's perfection thus offered we knew.
God's glorious great kingdom, clear here upon Earth,
His value proclaiming for all that it's worth.
Great Father of glory, dear Father of love,
The world's heaven sent beauty, Your gift from above.
A glimpsed sight of Heaven to behold and to share,
There's nowhere without Him could ever compare.

Sue O'Donnell

1

What's Love

To be given a hug that creates that
Feeling you hope will never end.

To have that warm feeling always with you
Knowing that they're always there to tend.

To look into their eyes and know
Everything is going to be alright.

To feel lost without them
Whenever they're out of sight.

To have someone to turn to who cares
When you've lost someone close to you.

And that person helping you overcome this
And put things back into a perspective view.

To laugh at each other and
Make each other smile.

To pick you up and spin you around
Just to act that little bit wild.

To meet someone and know
When together you're as one.

And to hope the day never comes
When one of you is gone.

Angela Wright

For Michelle

It's not just a word found in any Thesaurus
Nor chalked as graffiti on some school yard wall
No astrologers forecast for Libra or Taurus
No long dissertation or sermon to bore us
But with sweet exultation of angel-voiced chorus
A thing called 'love' touches the lives of us all.

It's not some obscure, abstract concept we've heard
Nor yet some vague notion perplexing the brain
No sepulchre wherein the heart is interred
And to view it as such would be simply absurd
It enables the spirit to soar like a bird
As our 'raison d'être' transcends the mundane.

There are those who would have us believe love is blind
There are others who say it's a gamble at best
Profuse are the ways in which love is defined
But the power of love cannot be undermined
For to love and be loved is in beauty enshrined
And when two hearts entwine each is more than twice blessed.

Love of country, of life, and a love of life's pleasure
Each holds its own place in the heart that beats true
But the greatest of loves, and the world's greatest treasure
Is the love that's committed, that knows no half measure
It sustains us through work and enriches our leisure
This eternally honest love I found with you.

Ron Beaumont

216

Love Memories

Memories warm, tender and sweet
When I played happily at my mother's feet
A mother's love so protective and pure
Always there for me of that I was sure.
A father's love strong, guiding and right
Taking care of me, morning till night
The love of a teacher who could see
With that extra encouragement what I could be.
True love of a friend through the years
Who shared my laughter, joy and tears.
Falling in love with my beloved, dear heart
The breaking of love when death did us part.
All of these loves are needed by us all
But many are not able to walk that tall.
There is a beautiful love above all other
It's the free gift of love from our heavenly Father.
Unlike other love it's always the same
It's for everyone who calls on His name.

Veronica Quainton

Lovers

Making love is like velvet
It's like rich, ruby wine.
It isn't dependent
On place or on time.

Making love links our bodies
It binds also our souls.
Each time is so different
As we each change our roles.

Making love can be gentle
It can also be rough.
It can say 'God I love you'
Or 'Help me life's tough'.

Making love can bring healing
It can also bring pain.
It can get you talking
And laughing again.

Making love is the ultimate
The pure giving game.
When you give me everything
And I do the same.

Danusia Wheeler

An Ordinary Lass

I was an ordinary lass,
no frills at all - that's me,
but all that changed when we first met,
when you gave your heart to me.

You made me feel so special,
like honey from a bee.
I felt I was in paradise
when you gave your heart to me.

You love filled me with pure delight,
my mind was all at sea,
your smile was like a lifebuoy,
when you gave your love to me.

As I stand here at the altar
in all my finery,
I'll gladly give my heart to you
as you gave your heart to me.

Peggy Gulliver

John And Teresa

He stands so tall with his woman at his side
With the love of his life, taking all in his stride
She turns towards him now,
And her eyes meet his gaze
Filled with admiration,
Loving all his ways.

What does he feel as his bride stands at his side?
Twenty-five years down the line, his heart still swells with pride
Teresa is his special gift
And love has grown so deep
A gift from God, so treasured
A gift from God to keep.

As Teresa turns to look at John, her heart then skips a beat
All down the years, his patient love and faithfulness does keep.
When other lives just fall apart
And love in them grows cold,
What is it keeps these two in love
Two lambs together in His fold?

Pilgrim in his journey, was shown a blazing fire
In front of which his enemy, poured water on, this his desire
To quench the fire, to put it out.
In room behind, a friend so true
Poured oil, and so those flames just grew!

A threefold cord is not easily broken
Jesus, to John and Teresa has spoken.
Since God is for them,
Who against them can prevail?
So with Jesus first, this marriage will not fail!

Chrissie Möller

The First Kiss

It's not because I bring your dinner on a tray.
It's not because when I say things need fixing, mending,
My words fall on deaf ears lending.
It's not because with aching back I pick up shoes,
Jackets and ties draped in twos.
It's not because you follow rugby,
Watch countless replays and never hug me.
It's just because at night time late,
I hear you enter through our gate.
You look at me then slowly smile,
Bleary now those navy-blue eyes.
You sit and reminisce about our first kiss
I have to smile, this ancient memory surfaces survives.
Shuffles the old coal of a fire burnt low.
Warms up my aching heart, I still love you so.

Ethel Oates

Alfie
(My first love)

Young Alfie was my sweetheart,
And lived next door but one.
He called for me each morning
And off to school we'd run.
He'd pass notes in the classroom,
And sometimes sweeties too,
And vowed to me, in his childish scrawl,
That he'd be forever true!
The idyllic years of childhood passed,
Our happiness complete,
Till the crunch of Alfie's Army boots
Went echoing down our street.
Then off he went, with his head erect,
Our country to defend,
Far away to the desert,
Where loving notes he penned.
Then suddenly his letters ceased -
My letters were returned -
Had he fallen on the battlefield
Or was my love now spurned?
Whoever could I turn to now
To help in my distress,
For his family had moved away
And left no forwarding address?
I languished on, in deep despair,
Till the war came to an end,
And then the stark news reached me -
He'd married my best friend!

Joan Leahy

Dream Lover

I love to be with you just talking;
I love to be with you just walking.
How could I go on without you,
Without seeing you at all?

Although I cannot matter much to you,
Or figure in your life at all,
In your world which is beyond me,
That is not for me to share,
Still far better to have it as it is,
Than to have you not at all.

For in my dreams you are my own;
In my dreams you love me;
There you are mine completely
And I am yours exclusively.

Megan Guest

Lovers

Love makes the world go round they say
And two lucky people will not gain say,
For Erika and Paul have a secret smile
Soon they'll be three but not for some while.

Hard work it will be and a house to get
Maybe St Jude will do his best yet,
If love and prayers can do the trick
They're home and dry and right in the thick.

A garden to keep, some nappies to wash
A job to do to earn lots of cash
The smile of a babe makes it all worthwhile
So watching and waiting with hope, that's the style.

M Ainsworth

Grant Me Access

Grant me access to your lips,
the rest of you, whatever expands
from our unity. Let your lips
spill words of wisdom, evolve

philosophies that overcome
the trivia of false perceptions.
Like expectations that deny you,
those devoid of openness. Let

all-embracing lips, such welcome
lips, speak beyond the fears and fads
of simple mores. Welcome the demand
for access; let whatever evolves

be yours to share.

Brian Blackwell

Poppy Love

How can it be that she has been sent
to love just me.
This gift from above
Is all that I love
I cherish thee
Dear Poppy.

How can it be that she has been sent
to love just me.
I have no answer to this
Since our first kiss
I know I just love thee
Dear Poppy.

Richard Phillips

Loving You

Just as
In the summer season
Of my life
The wind caresses
Your porcelain cheek
With loving whispers

So
In the winter of my days
When my frosted fingers
Creak and groan
To cross the ice floes
Of the creviced sheets
And my faint pulse
Does moan
So do I keep loving you.

John Crowe

Our Love

Love was in the air,
The night that I met you.
The moon shone so brightly
The stars from Heaven appeared.
It was a night I will remember
As I've remembered every night since.
Nights of passion, love, romance
Have filled our years together.

No longer in our youth today
Yet just as loving as ever.
Good times we've know - as well as bad
But we've come through together.

Our Diamond Day dawned yesterday
We're just as close as ever.

Janet Cavill

Heart, Body And Soul

I want you Mick, I need you so much
Since the night that we danced,
You felt warm to the touch.
You had your arms round me,
I felt safe and secure,
Now I'm yearning for you
With a love that's so pure.

You started to talk
But no response, did I speak,
Instead I just went back, and sat on my seat.
I should have told you how I felt,
I should have let you know
Of the burning hot passion, deep down within,
Making me fret with so much guilty and sin.

Now I'm approached by so many
But I have to say, 'No.'
You are the one I desire,
The one, who makes my heart glow,
I'll wait for you always,
                    Heart, body and soul.

Susan Senior

Before You

Before you there was me and now there is us,
The love you placed within my heart
Makes it feel like it will burst.
Burst with the sound of birds singing
On a beautiful sunlit spring morning;
Burst forth with the sight and smells
Of freshly opened flowers
Swaying in the morning breeze.
Burst with the enchantment of
The most wonderful arias.
You have set my heart and soul free
To soar above the dizzy heights
Of the Himalayan mountains,
Gazing through the keen eyes of a golden eagle
Looking down over God's grand creation.
Yes, before you, there was me.

Nick Cullen

First Kiss

Oh, what bliss
That first kiss
As we strolled along together.
He used to meet me on his bike
As I came home from school
He carried my bags
We often held hands
As we went along that summer.

A rose he'd bring me
As a token of love
We wandered along in a daze
We never imagined we'd ever part.
He had mine, I had his heart.

Then one day we disagreed
And went our separate ways
Never again to go through that phase
Of love's young dream,
But oh the bliss
Of that first kiss!

Peggy Smith

What Is Love?

Love is despair and desperation,
Longing and desire.
Fear, freedom and folly,
Cause to weep and reasons to be jolly.
Love brings Faith and Hope
Extends existing Charity.
Fills the mind, holds the heart
And gives to life a clarity.

Making things once masked
So sweet and clear,
And things once clear
Cloud over.
Be the reason to get up each day,
Perform each simple task
Find beauty in each thing which moves
Is a gift which has no parity.

To see the beauty in a leaf
And marvel at a spider's web;
Or be crushed like ice
On bended knees praying for release.
That is love, with all its faults
Fulfilments and desires,
Which makes a day worth living.
Or a night seem like Hell's fire.

Kay Reynolds

A Rainbow Of Emotion

The drums are pounding
Like a wild, tribal war dance,
Pulsating with a rhythmic passion
That deafens my ears.

A river meanders,
Cascading in the heartlands.
A rainbow of emotion
Amidst the waterfall spray.

Confusion reigns
As terrified natives scatter,
Seeking asylum, cocooned
In their own solitude.

A myriad of trumpets
Herald the arrival of a princess,
As waves of sunshine
Radiate from her smile.

As I dream of the moment
The songs of angels fly from her lips.

Kevin Connor

Kissing

There was a time
In late school age
When kissing
Was interesting
And strange

No two girls
Were quite alike
And some weren't right
Somehow
With clashing teeth
Or just a scent
That wasn't meant
For me

I held the moment
Kissed her still
As if kissing
Was thrilling

Confused inside
I could not say
It was less than that
For me

Dan Jakob

Untitled . . .

Love is something we cannot touch,
Only by giving can we show we care that much,
A tender look, a special glance,
Let love shine out, your life enhanced.

Tender new love takes time to grow,
And lifts one's spirits from feeling low,
Sincerity and trust are what you most need,
Don't let relationships go to seed.

Whatever you do, always be true,
With any acquaintance however old or new,
And love's full richness will come around,
Giving warmth to life, like a cloak surround.

Nicola Varmen

Lawns

We swore we'd love each other eternally   *(We didn't, of course)*
We vowed we'd never be parted   *(But you moved a few years later)*
We were so sure this was *it!*   *(But it wasn't!)*

We thought the long grass hid our indiscretions
                              (forgetting it swayed in the breeze)
We thought we were original and bold
                              (but our daring paths were others déjà vuex)
We though corn stood tall and golden forever
                              (forgetting that autumn and wind always come)

Ade Macrow

Wedding Day

Years of knowing each other
Love has truly grown
Now entering holy matrimony
You've exchanged your vows
Complete commitment shown
Handsome groom
Beautiful bride
Such a loving couple
Standing side by side
Mother and father
Families and all
Express their joy
Wish the bride and groom
True contentment evermore
From this day will always mean
A special day for you
God blessed your day
May He always in future
Matrimonial bliss
Congratulations as you celebrate
Your very happy event
This present moment.

Rosemary Sheridan

Endless Thoughts

I don't know the reason for it.
I don't know the reason why.
I just cannot get you out of my mind
No matter how hard I try.
I know when I go to bed tonight
Even though you're not really there
I know that as soon as I close my eyes
I can still see you everywhere.
Twenty-four hours, seven days a week
You're always in my head.
I'm sure I'll still have you in my thoughts
Even after when I'm dead.

Stephen Hibbeler

To My Lilly

For I am gone to Lilly, my love,
my Lilly, my Love, today
and the long road stealing upwards, onwards,
is the road that will brook no delay.

In her hills and her fields am I wandered
in her heart I am lost where I lay
for I am gone to my Lilly, my love,
my Lilly, my love today.

And did you see, and did you feel
the rain fall silent, and falling still?
A different wheel turns once, then twice
as my Lilly calls down from the hill.

My Lilly, my love, is a gracious suitor
sharp-carved from an unending quest
and she calls in imperial thunder
and she calls at her lady's behest.

And she calls in resonant voices
and she calls me now to obey.
For I have gone to my Lilly, my love,
my Lilly, my love today.

Peter Jones

Our Life

You are the rock on which I build,
The sea on which I sail.
Our world together is where I live
And where each day does pass.

North to south and east to west,
I know with me you will be,
Surrounded by happiness and love,
Throughout eternity.

   K Teasdale

The Enchantment

This enchanted dream awoke
The sunkist seed on sunglit scene
Warming where love's storm
Delighted in furious clasp
The unspoken embrace.

Above and below
The gentle murmur of water ripples
Translucently merged into the bubble
A symphonic diffusion into a perfect union

And you seal fragrance
Flower, leaf, bud and blossom
Bottle potion and orchestrate song
All that ought to belong
Where she silently watches
Her dream emblazoned in vibrancy
Accentuate the silent impale.

S Zartashia Al-Jalaly

Lights! Camera! Enter Spring!

Dark Winter's thoughts
fade as weather warms
of past withering plants
death of blossoms on the vine
& leaves crackling under
trampling boots.

So know ye all who think
of death – that it is but a cycle
of change & Spring is here
at last to prove me right.
Sprouts push their stems
through earth like green arrows
seeking sun. They bud before
your eyes just as the years grant
you life. Flowers bare their faces
shamelessly. Nature's colouring
providing cosmetic foundations.
Diversity flourishes everywhere.
Complexions vibrate to the sun –
quiver with life & sensuality.
Insects fly/crawl/buzz around
these rouged harlots crazed by
scents & juices. The dance of life
continues & love is rekindled
between lost lovers beneath
a beneficent Spring full moon.

Edward L Smith & Carmen M Pursifull